"This new book by Evan Carmichael, an authority on this topic, is exactly what you'll want to study. Written by a man who has been there, done that, and continues to do so with excellence, the lessons, stories, and remarkable insights he shares will take you step-by-step on a journey to success in both business and life."

—Bob Burg,
bestselling author of
The Go-Giver

"*Your One Word* is the real deal—a smart, actionable guide that empowers each of us to take control of our success, and make it our own. It all starts with just one word."

—Mel Robbins,
bestselling author, TEDx phenom, and CNN analyst

"Evan's passion for serving entrepreneurs is evident in all he does. I discovered this through his YouTube channel impacting millions of entrepreneurs monthly, but when I watched, it became no surprise why so many people follow him: his advice is solid, his experience is unmatched, and his heart for service makes for an amazing combo. Now I turn to Evan for help with my own business and every single time he delivers. Thanks, Evan!"

—Tim Schmoyer,
creator of Video Creators on YouTube

YOUR ONE WORD

YOUR ONE WORD

The Powerful Secret to Creating a
Business and Life That Matter

EVAN CARMICHAEL

A TarcherPerigee Book

tarcherperigee

An imprint of Penguin Random House LLC
375 Hudson Street
New York, New York 10014

Most TarcherPerigee books are available at special quantity discounts for bulk purchase for sales promotions, premiums, fund-raising, and educational needs. Special books or book excerpts also can be created to fit specific needs. For details, write: SpecialMarkets@penguinrandomhouse.com.

ISBN 9780143109099

Printed in the United States of America
1 3 5 7 9 10 8 6 4 2

All the great things are simple,
and many can be expressed in a single word.
—WINSTON CHURCHILL

CONTENTS

INTRODUCTION

A journey of a thousand miles begins with a
single step.
—*Lao-tzu (ancient Chinese philosopher,*
known as the founder of
philosophical Taoism)

IF YOU HAD ONE SHOT . . .

If you had one shot, or one opportunity to seize everything you ever
wanted. One moment. Would you capture it or just let it slip?
—*Eminem (rapper and bestselling US recording artist)*

"Evan, I paid you big money. I flew you halfway around the world to be
here today. You better make this audience come alive!"

Those were the words the organizer of the conference in Malaysia
said to me two minutes before I was due on stage to kick off his event.
Quite the pep talk.

Malaysia Social Media Week (MSMW) was a big deal. I walked
into the hall and could tell these guys meant it. Huge room. Giant
stage. Bright lights. High-end audiovisual gear. Cameras from every angle. Chairs filled the room and people were streaming in. For
the first time in a while I was *really* nervous. Eminem's lyrics were
in my head. I didn't want to let my shot slip. Somehow between the

jet lag and caffeine/sugar rush from a Frappuccino I steadied my nerves and told the organizer,

"Don't worry, Norman. I got this."

I'd gone to Malaysia to discuss a powerful secret I'd discovered and that changed my life, my business, and those of the entrepreneurs I'd introduced it to. Norman had reason to be worried, though. He'd asked me to come speak after seeing my YouTube videos. He liked my passion and wondered if I could pass it on to entrepreneurs in his country. In front of the largest audience MSMW had ever seen, senior government officials, some of the nation's top marketing influencers, and an international web audience, I was about to take the stage. If I didn't deliver, Norman would be on the hook for bringing this Canadian YouTuber to headline their event.

What happened next was amazing.

I got up and shared the One Word secret that had changed everything for me—and the audience loved it. Laptops were pounded on furiously with notes. The session was trending nationally on Twitter. The large screen keeping track of live interactions updated so quickly that you couldn't read it anymore. By the end of the hour people lined up, not to ask questions, but to take pictures with me. I went from unknown to rock star in sixty minutes. The best part was coming out and seeing Norman. He was smiling from ear to ear and gave me a bone-crushing handshake that seemed to last for days and a heartfelt message: "Thank you for helping us believe."

In this book I'm going to share that One Word secret to help transform you into a powerful force for good and help get you through your worst days.

THE WORST DAY OF MY LIFE

No one really has a bad life... Just bad moments.

—*Regina Brett* (New York Times
   bestselling author, newspaper columnist)

"Danny, I quit."

I couldn't believe those words were coming out of my mouth. All my life I grew up believing that you should never quit something that's important to you. My parents always told me that I was a Castrilli-Carmichael and could do anything, and here I was telling my business partner that I was done. Finito. Out.

I was over at my parents' house for dinner and took the call from Danny upstairs. The past year had been really hard. I'd turned away six-figure jobs to do my own business, and ended up making only three hundred dollars a month and not being able to survive. When my friends invited me out for birthdays or dinners, I had to say no. I told them I was busy working on my business, but the reality was that I couldn't afford the twenty dollars the evening would cost, and I was too embarrassed to tell them that I didn't have any money. I mean, here I was, turning down jobs they wanted so I could live the entrepreneur's dream. How could I tell them the truth? I felt like a huge fraud.

So Danny, my business partner, wanted to talk. We disagreed on what to do next in the business. I felt like we had tried everything, and nothing was working out. I'd had success with everything I'd ever applied myself to: school, sports, piano lessons . . . If I worked harder, I would get better. And here I was pouring every ounce of strength I had, putting every waking moment, and every single dollar, into a business that wasn't working. I felt hopeless. My once sky-high self-confidence was in the toilet. Enough was enough. I couldn't take it anymore.

So I quit.

Then I cried.

Uncontrollably.

I cried so hard I didn't know what was coming out of my eyes and what was coming out of my nose. I'm not one who cries much, but I didn't know what else to do. I felt like everything I'd worked on, everything I'd believed in, everything I'd loved had just been taken away from me. My mother, hearing me sobbing, came upstairs, put her hands on my shoulders, and tried to comfort me. I have no idea what she said. I couldn't hear it. I was too lost.

I went to bed and hoped better days were ahead.

TIME TO RISE

Our greatest glory is not in never falling, but in rising every time we fall.

—*Confucius (philosopher and founder of Confucianism)*

I woke up the next day and asked myself, "What do I want to do with my life?"

If money wasn't a concern . . . If I could do anything I wanted . . . If I had no restrictions . . . what would I do? It didn't take me long to figure out that if I could do anything, I would get back into my business.

If you're doing something just to make money, it's easy to quit. Most people do. But if you're doing something because it makes you come alive, then removing the restrictions life throws at you clears the path.

I didn't want to live in regret for the rest of my life, wondering what would have happened if I had just gotten up for one more day and kept running my company.

I didn't want to go take a job I knew I didn't love, hoping one day to get back to my business while digging myself further and further into a corporate world I didn't know if I'd be able to get out of.

I had to find a way to keep going with my business.

The optimist in me took over. I didn't know how it was going to work out. We had no evidence that what we were doing would work. I was making three hundred dollars a month, for crying out loud! But I had to believe it would.

I got dressed, made my lunch (lunch was always canned beans with olive oil and herbs—it was all I could afford), and headed over to my partner's apartment as I usually did. He had a small condo that functioned as our "corporate headquarters." He worked in his den, which was too small for both of us to fit in, so I worked at his dining room table.

The entire way there I was nervous. I had just quit on him the night before, and now here I was, coming back to work. I didn't know how he would react. Maybe he'd call me a traitor or a deserter. Maybe he wouldn't let me back in. At best, I was expecting an awkward conversation. At worst, I would be out. But I had to find out.

He opened the door and looked me right in the eyes. I looked back at him. To my surprise, he didn't bring anything up. We just dove back into our work. He understood how stressful this business was and cut me a huge amount of slack.

I had hit my bottom and needed to find a way to get momentum.

WHY I WROTE THIS BOOK

When you have that window of opportunity called a crisis, move as quickly as you can, get as much done as you can. There's a momentum for change that's very compelling.

—Anne M. Mulcahy (former chairperson and CEO of Xerox Corporation)

I wrote this book to give *you* momentum.

I made it through. I went from having an income below the poverty line to signing NASA and Johnson & Johnson as clients. We had customers in more than thirty countries. Within three years of my "I quit!" moment, we built and sold our company, and I moved on to other businesses, investments, and adventures. I almost didn't make it, but, thankfully, I did.

And I want you to as well.

I wrote this book because 80 percent of start-ups fail. Because chances are you've had moments when you cried your guts out over your company. Because you've told yourself or your business partner that you quit. Because you've doubted yourself and felt like you should be doing way better, making way more money, and having a way bigger impact on the world.

Just like I did.

Every time I meet entrepreneurs who are struggling to get their businesses to where they want them to be, I think back to that night at my parents' house when my dream fell apart, when I couldn't understand how I could be pouring my heart into this idea and not be getting any momentum, when I felt completely lost, hopeless, and worthless.

I don't want you to go through that.

Entrepreneurs feed my soul. If you're trying to do something important and need help, I could sit, chat, talk, e-mail, video call with you all day long. It's part of who I am. If someone gave me a million dollars with the condition that I could never talk with entrepreneurs again, I wouldn't take it. I bleed with you.

But my time isn't scalable. Like you, I only have twenty-four hours in my day. My personal goal is to help one billion entrepreneurs, and my hope is that even if I never get the opportunity to meet you in person, this book will help give you the momentum, guidance, and confidence you need to build a business and life you can be proud of.

I want you to find and live your One Word. I want your entrepreneurial dreams to come true.

ARE YOU A DREAMER?

If you dream it, you can do it.

—*Walt Disney (entrepreneur, cartoonist, animator, voice actor, film producer, and cofounder of the Walt Disney Company)*

Your One Word can help you turn your dreams into reality.

Some have used the ideas in this book to build *multibillion*-dollar businesses. I'm going to give you the surprisingly simple yet powerful formula that they used and you can use to realize your dreams.

Here are some of the stories you'll learn from in this book:

- How Louis Trahan turned a one-page concept into **over $10 million in sales.**
- How Christopher Gavigan took the Honest Company from zero to hundreds of millions in revenue and a **$1 billion valuation** in three years.
- How Dheeraj Pandey created a **$2 billion company** in a boring, unsexy industry that nobody wanted to talk about.

These entrepreneurs, and many others, all used their One Word to solve big problems, create massive wealth, and have a significant worldly impact.

But you don't need to have a lot of money, be a celebrity, or be influential to find and then apply your One Word.

You might be thinking that you don't want to build a multibillion-dollar business. You just want to provide a steady income for your family and get out of debt.

Using your One Word works just as well to help you make $5,000 as it does to help you make $5 billion.

You can apply this strategy to:

- Coming up with a business idea, finding your first customer, raising start-up funding, creating a word-of-mouth campaign, getting the media to talk about you, landing angel and venture capital money, securing important partnerships, opening up international opportunities, hiring your first employee, building a lasting and meaningful culture, making the world a better place, and more.

I'm giving you a tool to help you make decisions more easily, keep you motivated, and allow others to spread your message for you.

Now it's your turn. Let's get started!

BREAKDOWN

The mind is the limit. As long as the mind can envision the fact that you can do something, you can do it.

—Arnold Schwarzenegger (actor, producer, former professional bodybuilder, and politician)

You've never read a book like this.

The powerful secret in this book is open to you. It will help you make sense of your business, your decisions, and your search for meaning. It will help you unlock your potential and create a new world that you didn't know existed. You'll have the motivation, purpose, and understanding you need to finally achieve your goals and do something important.

It's divided into three parts: Core, Campaign, and Company.

In part 1, **CORE,** you will *discover your greatness* and learn how to apply it to make money and make a difference. You'll learn about the *One Word philosophy* and the powerful *Core Selling technique*. You'll understand how I used my One Word to *start a movement* and how other successful entrepreneurs have built empires worth billions of dollars using theirs. Finally you'll learn how to unlock your potential and find your One Word.

In part 2, **CAMPAIGN,** you're ready to take your One Word and start to apply it to create a campaign for your business. *Something people will care about.* You'll learn how to get all the pieces in place to launch your campaign, and we will run through *a checklist* of everything you'll need to get started. You'll also find *case studies* and expertise culled from interviews with those leaders and an action plan modeled after my own *#Believe campaign*.

In part 3, **COMPANY,** I'll show you *how to use your One Word* and apply it to different components of building a business, including *raising capital, marketing and branding, customer service, recruiting a team and building a culture, and operations*. I'll include real-world examples from successful entrepreneurs who are using One Word to build meaningful businesses and show you how you can model their success.

This book will challenge your thinking.

It'll force you to reexamine your beliefs and the way you see the world. It'll stretch your comfort zone. And it can make you a world influencer. Buckle up. You're about to go on a life-changing adventure. I'm excited for you!

#Believe.

COMING UP: *In chapter 1, I'll show you how you can find your greatness and the impact that your One Word can have.*

CORE

I think it's very important not to do what your peers think you should do, not do what your parents think you should do, or your teachers or even your culture. *Do what's inside of you.*
—*George Lucas (billionaire entrepreneur and*
  creator of Star Wars *and* Indiana Jones)

IN PART 1: CORE, you will *discover your greatness* and learn how to apply it to make money and make a difference. You'll learn about the *One Word philosophy* and the powerful *Core Selling technique*. You'll understand how I used my One Word to *start a movement* and how other successful entrepreneurs have built empires worth billions of dollars using theirs. Finally you'll learn how to unlock your potential and find your One Word.

CHAPTER 1

ONE WORD IMPACT

If you think you're too small to have an impact, try going to bed with a mosquito.

*—Anita Roddick (founder of the Body Shop
and pioneer of ethical consumerism)*

IS YOUR LIFE MEDIOCRE?

Ninety percent of America gets up in the morning
and drives to a job they hate.

—Dana White (president of the Ultimate Fighting Championship)

Please sit down and let's have an honest talk.

Most people live mediocre lives.

You wake up and drive to a job you don't love, so you can work with a team that doesn't support you, and do tasks that are beneath your skill level.

You never achieve greatness. You never accomplish your dreams. You never make a big impact on the world.

You're living for the evenings and weekends, and hope that the time spent working just doesn't suck too much.

You may have been told that you're not good enough.

You may think you don't have the resources to follow your true passion.

You may be afraid to try something new after starting down one path.

And, hey, you've got mouths to feed, responsibilities to look after, and not enough savings. You just can't afford to take a risk.

The saddest news of all is that you've set the bar so low for yourself that you've created a world where it's okay to be mediocre.

You've created an environment of thinking small and being insignificant.

You want to do more, act more, be more, but something is holding you back.

The people you hang out with, the websites you visit, the media you consume—everything in your environment holds you exactly where you are.

It prevents you from taking steps forward.

Being mediocre has not only become acceptable but is the norm. Because it's comfortable. Because it's safe. But it's limiting you.

I want you to do something important with your life and stop being mediocre.

BEING MEDIOCRE IS INSULTING

Everything about mediocrity kills me.

—Ivanka Trump (former model and American entrepreneur)

If you care about your life, then being mediocre should be insulting.

At the risk of offending you, I'm using strong language intentionally. This has to be important to you. If it's important, then you'll change. If it's important, you'll make it a priority. If it's important, you'll face your fears. If it's important, you'll stop making excuses.

When something is truly, deeply important to you, you find ways to make it happen, even when the #LittleMan (see p. 117) tells you it's not possible.

If it's not important enough to you, then you won't do anything about it. You'll continue doing exactly what you're doing now. Being mediocre is easy. Anybody can do it. And most people and companies do.

Following your passion, being crazy enough to try to change the world, and standing for something important are hard.

So most people and companies don't, and thus most businesses are mediocre too.

They're boring and uninspiring. You haven't made people care enough about what you're doing. I mean really care. Feel-it-in-their-bones care. Tell-all-their-friends-about-you care. Tattoo-your-logo-on-their-body care. Even if you get halfway to that level of care, you'll be way ahead of your competition.

Right now if someone lowers their prices by 10 percent, you lose your customers. Because everyone is selling the same products and services. Because there really isn't all that much that separates you from your competition. There is no strong customer loyalty because you're not inspiring it. And, hey, you're not alone.

The Fortune 500 list was first created in 1955. Only 13 percent of the companies on that original list are still on the list today.

Thirteen percent! The others faded away because they were boring and lost relevancy.

Most businesses are boring.

Do you want to know the first step to having a remarkable business? Here's where it all begins and your life and business will change forever:

You need to find your greatness.

FIND YOUR GREATNESS

Greatness is not this wonderful, esoteric, elusive, god-like feature that only the special among us will ever taste. It's something that truly exists in all of us.

—*Will Smith (actor and entrepreneur)*

Do you have the mindset for greatness?

This isn't hokey, fluffy, BS advice.

If you're laughing at this point, or are about to close the book or think you know better, then you need this chapter more than anyone else.

You're not hitting your big goals and you picked up this book for a reason, so at least give yourself a chance and finish this section. All the advice and books in the world will be useless to you until you fix your mindset.

Your limiting mindset is holding you where you are.

One of the most powerful ads Nike has ever created doesn't feature Michael Jordan or LeBron James. It pictures a chubby kid huffing and puffing as he's running down an open road. To see a copy of the ad check out evancarmichael.com/oneword/extras.

Nike's ads usually feature great athletes—physical specimens at the peak of their careers who have already achieved extraordinary success.

And here is this fat kid . . . running . . . and he's . . . great?

Yes, because he took the first step. He started doing.

YOU START AT THE START

Start by doing what's necessary; then do what's possible; and suddenly you are doing the impossible.

—Francis of Assisi (Italian Roman Catholic friar and preacher, and one of the most respected religious figures in history)

Whoever made this ad for Nike is a genius and needs a raise.

This ad speaks directly to your mindset for greatness.

When you're finding your greatness, you start at the beginning. Everyone starts at the beginning. And the beginning is really hard. Just taking the first step is hard. Maybe this kid wants to be a distance runner and win an Olympic medal. He tells his friends and family and they all laugh at him.

Classic #LittleMan behavior.

"You want to what? Umm . . . have you looked at yourself in the mirror?"

This fat kid is *you*.

You have a big goal and you're just getting started on it. You don't have the skills. You don't have the training. You don't have the experience. You don't have all the answers. So you're going to make a lot of mistakes and you won't make very much progress right away.

The difference is going to be *how* you see yourself when you look in the mirror. Do you honestly, deep down, see a future Olympic runner?

Or do you just see a fat kid?

If you just see a fat kid staring back at you, then you'll never reach your goals until you change your mindset. Maybe your first run is only to the edge of your driveway. That's okay. Most people quit here. *"It's too hard. I'll never make it. What was I thinking? Man, this was a stupid idea."*

Understand that every successful person was once this fat kid when they got started. And as with any skill, they learned, practiced, and got better. Consistently. They found their greatness. They didn't let the #LittleMan hold them back. They believed in themselves. So they succeeded.

What do you see in the mirror?

If you see greatness, you're ready for your One Word.

THE SECRET: YOUR ONE WORD

Better than a thousand hollow words,
is one word.

—*Buddha (sage whose teachings*
   founded Buddhism)

I'm going to share a secret with you.

A secret so powerful that once you discover it, every decision you make in your life and business will become easier.

Doors will start to open where before you struggled to make any progress. You'll finally feel like you're living your life with a purpose instead of fighting the world around you.

Great leaders have used this secret to build powerful companies, spark important movements, and create meaningful change.

And now you can too.

Here's the secret: There is One Word that defines who you are.

There is One Word that connects all the things in your life that make you come alive. Think about the friends you have, the music you listen to, the books you read, the movies you watch, the companies you've worked for, the businesses you've started. Think about everything in your life right now that you enjoy.

They are all connected.

Until you figure out what that connection is, you'll never live up to your potential.

What's your favorite song? And what does it have to do with who your best friend or favorite book is?

The answer is everything. And it can be boiled down to one simple, powerful word.

Great people can be described in One Word.

Martin Luther King Jr.: *Equality.* Oprah Winfrey: *Heart.* Steve Jobs: *Impact.* You: *?*

If you want to break free from the chains of mediocrity and really make an impact, then it starts with finding your One Word.

You have to stand for something powerful and important.

STAND FOR SOMETHING

Faith is taking the first step even when you don't see the whole staircase.

—Martin Luther King Jr. (pastor, activist, humanitarian, and leader in the civil rights movement)

On August 23, 1963, a quarter of a million people went to Washington, DC, to hear Martin Luther King Jr. speak at the Lincoln Memorial.

How did he get so many people to come out?

He didn't have a newsletter or a Twitter account. He wasn't making YouTube videos or using Google AdWords. He didn't have a website or use Facebook. He didn't have any of the tools that make it so easy for us today to reach people and start movements.

And yet 250,000 people came out. Why?

Because he stood for something important.

The cause he believed in touched people's hearts and led them to action. It was so important that people willingly spread the word and promoted his cause—because it was their cause.

You need to do the same.

What does this have to do with business?

You might be thinking, "That's great, it works for political or cultural movements but what does this have to do with business?" I'm glad you asked.

What we're talking about here is getting people to take action—influencing decision making by appealing to something that people feel passionate about. It can apply to going to your website and buying your product just as easily as it does to getting in a bus and traveling to hear Martin Luther King Jr. speak.

Most companies just never do it (see previous notes on mediocrity). Your business is not just about making a product or service. That's a recipe for failure.

People want to know who you are and what you stand for before they'll buy anything from you. It's about standing for something important and having your cause be your customers' cause.

Let me introduce you to Core Selling.

CORE SELLING

A mediocre idea that generates enthusiasm will go further than a great idea that inspires no one.

—*Mary Kay Ash (founder of Mary Kay Cosmetics)*

This concept alone will transform your business and how you market yourself.

There are three kinds of selling in business: *feature*, *benefit*, and *core*.

1. **Feature Selling**

   When you first start selling something you usually promote its features.

   You're talking about the specifics of what your company offers.

   Here are some examples of feature-based selling:

   - These sheets have a thread count of twelve hundred.
   - This car has a fuel economy of thirty-four miles per gallon.
   - This lightbulb will last ten years.

2. **Benefit Selling**

   Somewhere along the way you learn from reading a book, watching a video, or talking with others that you should be selling benefits, not features.

   You tell me not just what your product or service does, but how I'm going to gain from using it. Sell the hole, not the drill.

   Benefit-based selling would change the sales pitches to:

   - These sheets are super soft and you'll get a great night's sleep.
   - You'll save a lot of money on gas with this car and rarely have to fill up.
   - You'll never have to change a lightbulb again!

Feature and benefit selling are how 99 percent of the world sells today. It works but it's inefficient.

3. **Core Selling**

   Forget features and benefits. The real gold is in Core Selling. In Core Selling you lead with your One Word. What are you here to do? Why is this so important?

Let me show you an example.

#CALM

The "flower guy" selling "calm" was a lightbulb flash exploding in my brain.

—*Wayne E. (One of Evan's YouTube subscribers)*

A subscriber, Jay, wrote to tell me that he wants to start a flower shop and asked me how he could stand out.

Now, the flower industry is brutal. Ridiculously brutal. Margins are being squeezed by supermarkets and online stores. There are fewer flower growers, making it harder to find locally grown products. It's one of the most competitive online businesses, so good luck with getting people to search and find your website. When the economy is down, luxury items like flowers are the first thing people stop spending money on. The big referral partners, like funeral parlors and banquet halls, already have long-standing relationships with florists. Man . . . who wants to be in the flower business? Jay did. So I was going to help him.

The secret was for Jay to realize that he wasn't selling flowers.

He was selling something much more powerful. Jay was really selling #Calm. What I learned from Jay was that he loves flowers because they make him feel calm. If he is stressed or worried, he looks at flowers and becomes calm. That's his core. For Jay to avoid massive failure and beat the odds, he needed to embrace #Calm.

And it's so much more than just having great flowers.

His store should be a haven for people who want to feel calm. He should sell flowers that make people calm. He should have signage outside that makes people calm. He should play music, hire staff, greet people, fill the air with scents, and have a store layout that makes people calm. He should get involved with charities that help people deal with stress and overcoming trauma. Talking with Jay or anyone on his team should make you feel calm. For him to be successful, he needs others to experience the calm feeling that he loves getting from his flowers.

And it's easy to do. It doesn't have to be faked. It's not just a marketing strategy. Because that's who Jay is. He just needs to embrace it and share it. Then his flower shop will become a destination for people who want to be calm. He'll attract people he'll naturally get along with, who will buy more flowers, spend more money, refer more customers, and won't compare him to the dozen roses you can buy online for $19.99.

That's Core Selling. And it applies to much more than just selling. It's a philosophy for how to run your entire business and your life. Almost nobody does it, and it's your chance to dominate your industry.

It's also how to make lots of money.

HOW TO MAKE MONEY

If you just work for money, you'll never make it, but if you love what you're doing, success will be yours.

—*Ray Kroc (built McDonald's and his family fortune is worth billions of dollars)*

"I want to make a million dollars before I turn X years old."
Sound familiar?

Most new entrepreneurs are just trying to make money.

And that's why they fail.

You're tired of working for someone else and think you can strike it rich by branching off on your own.

You're partly right.

If you look at any list of the world's wealthiest people and remove those who had inherited wealth, almost everyone else is an entrepreneur.

You don't make real money working for someone else.

But . . . and this is a *huge* "but". . .

If money is your only goal, then you'll never be rich.

Look at the list of the most successful entrepreneurs and you'll see that none of them are driven by the money.

They want to **change the way something is done.**

They want to have an **impact.**

They want to leave a **legacy.**

To be successful as an entrepreneur, you need to build a business around your passion and use your One Word as your operating philosophy.

You're not running a charity here (unless you are). Money is important. You're here to create profits and wealth. But it's not the most important thing.

Let me show you how Steve Jobs got rich.

HOW STEVE JOBS GOT RICH

I was worth over a million dollars when I was 23, over $10 million when I was 24 and over $100 million when I was 25. But you know what? The money wasn't that important. I wasn't in it for the money.

—*Steve Jobs (billionaire entrepreneur and cofounder of Apple Computer)*

Steve Jobs wanted to "put a dent in the universe."

He had all the money he'd ever need for the rest of his life when he was in his early twenties.

He could have retired, partied, traveled the world, bought a professional sports team—anything!

And what did he do?

He continued to work at Apple.

Until the day he died, Steve Jobs worked on projects that would help him put a dent in the universe.

You might be thinking: "That's great, Evan. Give me $1 billion and I'll go put a dent in the universe, as well."

And that's exactly why you're not successful.

Yet.

Steve Jobs didn't make his billions and then want to have an impact.

It's because he wanted to have an impact that he made his billions.

Is this sinking in yet?

The core comes first and the money follows.

And it's not just Steve Jobs.

This is a pattern used by the world's most successful entrepreneurs. You can use it too and achieve beyond your wildest goals.

Your mindset for greatness leads to your One Word so that you're standing for something important, you're Core Selling, and you're making a lot of money.

This is the root cause of entrepreneurial success.

SUCCESS LEAVES CLUES

> If you want to be successful, find someone who has achieved the results you want and copy what they do and you'll achieve the same results.
>
> —*Tony Robbins (life coach, self-help author, and motivational speaker)*

Still don't believe that money should never be your primary goal? Here are some more examples to follow (emphasis mine). I encourage you to look up your favorite entrepreneurs and see how they got started and where their priorities were.

> *Never go into business purely to make money.* If that's the sole motive . . . you're better off doing nothing.
>
> —*Richard Branson (billionaire founder of Virgin Group)*

> You have to be committed, and you have to find something that you are passionate about. And *forget about money.*
>
> —*Chris Gardner (went from homeless to millionaire, his story is told in the movie* The Pursuit of Happyness)

> If a man goes into business with only the idea of making a lot of money, chances are he won't. But if he puts service and quality first, *the money will take care of itself.* Producing a first-class product that is a real need is a much stronger motivation for success than getting rich.
>
> —*Joyce Clyde Hall (founder of Hallmark)*

> What I know is, is that if you do work that you love, and work that fulfills you, the rest will come. And I truly believe that the reason I've been able to be so financially successful is because *my focus has never, ever for one minute been money.*
>
> —*Oprah Winfrey (billionaire entrepreneur and creator of* The Oprah Winfrey Show)

Disneyland is a work of love. *We didn't go into Disneyland just with the idea of making money.*

—Walt Disney (entrepreneur, cartoonist, animator, voice actor,
  film producer, and cofounder of the Walt
  Disney Company)

The most important thing in life is to love what you're doing because that's the only way you'll ever be really good at it . . . *Money was never a motivation for me,* except as a way to keep score. The real excitement is playing the game.

—Donald Trump (billionaire business magnate, investor, television
  personality, and author)

If you focus on the money, you're not going to get anywhere. You can want to be successful, but at the end of the day, if money is your motivation, if that's how shallow your outlook is on life, then you're going to be such an empty person. Because there's nothing driving you from the inside—there's no passion.

—Jennifer Lopez (actress, author, fashion designer, dancer, producer, and
  singer worth over $250 million)

CHAPTER 1 HIGHLIGHTS

IMPORTANT TAKEAWAYS

- Don't do what the people around you think you should do. Do what's inside you.
- Most people live mediocre lives and have set the bar so low that they've created a world where it's okay to be mediocre.

- The people you hang out with, the websites you visit, the media you consume, everything in your environment holds you exactly where you are.
- The Fortune 500 list was first created in 1955. Only 13 percent of the companies on the original list are still on it today.
- You need to find your greatness.
- Everyone starts at the start. The difference is where you see yourself going.
- There is One Word that defines who you are, connects all the things in your life that make you come alive, and will you help escape the chains of mediocrity.
- People want to know who you are and what you stand for before they'll buy anything from you. Make your cause be your customer's cause too.
- Forget features and benefits. They work, but they're not efficient. The real gold is in Core Selling.
- Making money is so much more than just having a great product or service. It's about how you make people feel when they see your brand.
- If money is your only goal, then you'll never be rich. You have to want to have an impact and leave a legacy.
- Steve Jobs didn't make billions and then want to have an impact. It's because he wanted to have an impact that he made his billions.
- Never go into a business purely to make money. If that's the motive, you're better off doing nothing.

COMING UP: *In chapter 2, I'll share how I found my One Word and how it helped my business explode.*

MY ONE WORD, "BELIEVE"

Don't limit yourself. Many people limit themselves to what they think they can do. *You can go as far as your mind lets you.* What you believe, remember, you can achieve."

—*Mary Kay Ash (founder of Mary Kay Cosmetics)*

GNOTHI SEAUTON?

You can be pursuing a profession because your parents say it's the best thing. You can be pursuing a profession because you think you will make a lot of money. You can be pursuing a profession because you think you are going to get a lot of attention. None of that will do you any good if you are not being honest with yourself.

—*Oprah Winfrey (billionaire entrepreneur and creator of* The Oprah Winfrey Show)

Most people waste their lives living someone else's dream.

They imprison themselves by accepting the results of other people's thinking.

They allow the opinions of others to crush their own inner voice. You might have been beaten down so often that now you stomp out your own dreams before they even have a chance to blossom. You have become your own #LittleMan.

It's time to rediscover yourself.

The ancient Greeks had a proverb *gnothi seauton*, "know thyself."

It was used as a warning to pay no attention to the opinion of the masses.

It's a valuable reminder that this is your life.

You need to take charge.

If you want success . . .

If you want to accomplish your goals . . .

If you want your life to mean something and to have a significant impact . . .

You start by digging deep, to know yourself, to find your One Word, and to set your course in a powerful new direction.

For some people it's really easy and they get it right away.

For others, like myself, it takes time, analysis, and exercises to narrow it down.

If you don't do a lot of regular self-reflection, this will be a challenging activity—but totally worth it.

When I found my One Word, it changed my business and my life.

MY STORY OF #BELIEVE

When you believe a thing, believe it all the way, implicitly and unquestionably.

—Walt Disney (entrepreneur, cartoonist, animator, voice actor, film producer, and cofounder of the Walt Disney Company)

I was unhappy.

I started my business because I wanted to help entrepreneurs. I struggled so much to get my first business off the ground and almost gave up. One of the worst days of my life was when I told my business partner "I quit."

I was tired of putting in all this time and effort and money, and not seeing results. I was tired of working for less than minimum wage. I was tired of losing respect for myself and feeling like a total failure.

I managed to pull through, beat the odds, and be one of the success stories. And I wanted to share my experience and advice with others, because I almost didn't make it. I wanted to make their path a little easier than what I had to go through.

But I was unhappy.

I was unhappy because I started doing all sorts of different projects—a website, YouTube videos, radio shows, media interviews, and so on—but I wasn't getting people talking about my business enough.

It seemed too scattered. People couldn't wrap their heads around what I did, because it was all over the place.

I needed clarity.

I thought it was a marketing problem, so I met with my friend Jason to try to come up with a tagline for my business.

Over the years it has gone from "HELPING you build the company of your dreams" to "Motivation and strategies for entrepreneurs" to "Over 20 million entrepreneurs helped and counting."

Weak sauce.

What we came up with was "Hungry entrepreneurs deserve help." This felt better, but still wasn't quite right. Something was missing, and I couldn't put my finger on it.

Then Steve Jobs changed my life.

STEVE JOBS'S GREATEST SPEECH

Marketing is too important to be left to the marketing department.
—*David Packard (cofounder of Hewlett-Packard)*

One day I stumbled upon what would become one of my favorite YouTube videos of all time.

It was Steve Jobs talking about marketing. It hit on exactly what I was missing—the Core Selling that made Apple so successful. It's had a dramatic impact on my business and my life.

Here is part of what Steve said:

> *To me . . . marketing is about values. This is a very complicated world. It's a very noisy world. And we're not going to get a chance to get people to remember much about us. No company is! And so, we have to be really clear on what we want them to know about us. . . . The way to do that is NOT to talk about speeds and feeds. It's NOT to talk about bits and megahertz. It's NOT to talk about why we are better than Windows.*
>
> *. . . The best example of all, and one of the greatest jobs of marketing that the universe has ever seen, is Nike. Remember, Nike sells a commodity. They sell shoes!!!*
>
> *And yet, when you think of Nike you feel something different than a shoe company. In their ads, as you know, they don't ever talk about the product. They don't ever tell you about their air soles and why they are better than Reebok's air soles.*
>
> *What does Nike do in their advertising? They honor great athletes. And they honor great athletics. That's who they are, that's what they are about! And what we're about isn't making boxes for people to get their jobs done. . . . Apple is about something more than that!*
>
> *Apple at the core, its core value, is that we believe that*

people with passion can change the world for the better. That's what we believe!

And we believe that, in this world, people can change it for the better. And that those people who are crazy enough to think that they can change the world are the ones that actually do! . . . Values and core values—those things shouldn't change. The things that Apple believed in at its core are the same things Apple really stands for today.

To see the full video of his speech check out evancarmichael .com/oneword/extras.

Jobs ends his talk by saying that lots of things have changed—in the world, in the tech business, and at Apple. But that Apple's core values haven't changed—and that they're what the company needs to put forward to customers.

HOW YOU CAN MODEL STEVE JOBS

I think there is probably no better person to aspire to emulate than Steve Jobs and what he has done at Apple in terms of his leadership, his innovation, not settling for mediocrity.

—*Howard Schultz (billionaire chairman of Starbucks)*

If you act on what Steve Jobs said, you'll spark a movement.
This speech was given just after Steve Jobs returned to Apple.
In his absence, Apple had struggled.
It was a few months away from bankruptcy, had only 4 percent market share, and was losing over $1 billion a year.
Asking Jobs to come back was a "desperation" move.
Apple had just been through three different CEOs and nobody could make it work.
Jobs agreed and took his company from life support to being

the most valuable company in the world. It might be the single greatest turnaround story of all time.

It's time for your business to start taking off too.

In this speech, Jobs outlines the basics of Core Selling.

"The way to do that is NOT to talk about speeds and feeds. It's NOT to talk about bits and megahertz" = Feature Selling.

"It's NOT to talk about why we are better than Windows . . . And what we're about isn't making boxes for people to get their jobs done—although we do that well" = Benefit Selling.

"Marketing is about values . . . We have to be really clear on what we want them to know about us . . . Apple at the core, its core value, is that we believe that people with passion can change the world for the better. That's what we believe! . . . And we believe that, in this world, people can change it for the better. And that those people who are crazy enough to think that they can change the world, are the ones that actually do!" = Core Selling.

Mind. Blown.

I finally had some clarity. It was time to get to work.

CLARITY LEADS TO CONVICTION

> The beauty is that through disappointment you can gain clarity, and with clarity comes conviction and true originality.
>
> —Conan O'Brien (television host, comedian, writer, producer best known for hosting several late-night talk shows)

If you want to model Steve Jobs's amazing results, you need to get just as clear about who you are and what you stand for.

Once you have clarity, everything else falls into place.

I was frustrated that my business didn't have enough momentum and I didn't have the clarity I needed to move forward.

So I made a list, to try to find my core value.

I started with my "Hungry entrepreneurs deserve help" tagline and wrote down ideas for how to convey the emotion behind my work.

Something that really got my blood pumping.

I purposely tried not to think too much and instead just started writing whatever entered my mind. Here's what I came up with:

- Hungry entrepreneurs deserve help
- What I do . . . what I believe . . . but not inspirational
- Entrepreneurs change the world
- Entrepreneurs are heroes
- Celebrate entrepreneurs
- Rallying call
- Gets your heart pumping
- It's on you
- Take your shot
- Believe
- Follow your passion
- Overcome
- Persevere
- Keep going
- Step up
- Don't settle
- Start

I didn't love anything on the list yet. Nothing felt quite right—yet.

So I decided to sleep on it.

SLEEP ON IT

Sleep is the best meditation.

—Dalai Lama (head monk of the Gelug school, the newest of the schools of Tibetan Buddhism, and Nobel Peace Prize winner)

If you're struggling to make a decision, sleep on it and see how you feel in the morning.

I felt inspired by Steve Jobs and was ready to act but was frustrated that I couldn't get my clarity. I wanted it badly but it wasn't coming. **So I slept on it.** I came back to the same list the next day, and one word jumped out: "Believe." It was right there in the middle of my list. I thought about what "believe" meant to me. I came up with this:

- Believe in what you're doing—passion
- Believe that you can do it—confidence
- Believe that it will work—conviction

Finally, because I felt "Believe" on its own was too simple, I started looking for ways to add to it:

- Believe you can
- Believe in the possible
- Believe more
- Believe it all
- Believe in belief
- Believe and believe

The more I looked at the list, the more I realized that I just liked "Believe," so I decided that I was going to do this crazy thing and rebrand my entire business around "Believe."

It felt right . . . and my life was about to change.

THIS IS YOUR NEW WAY OF LIFE

The Macintosh is not a computer, it's a way of life.

—Don Rittner (historian, archeologist, environmental activist, educator, and author)

The one thing that hit me pretty quickly was that this was more than just a slogan.

This was a value. This was a personal mission statement. **This was a way of life. "Believe" became #Believe.** It started my movement. I looked back at the people I had hired on my team and the ones who were still with me were the ones who also had #Believe as a core value. I reflected on my personal life and realized that I've always been about believing, but I never realized it. I loved reading books about the little guy who overcame the odds to be successful. My favorite movie is *Seabiscuit*, which is the story of an undersized racehorse whose victories lifted a nation in the middle of the Great Depression. My favorite entrepreneur is A. P. Giannini, the founder of Bank of America, who made loans of as little as twenty-five dollars to people whose only collateral was the calluses on their hands. He would lend money based on "a man's face and a signature." My friends are about #Believe. The songs I like are about #Believe. Everything that makes me come alive somehow relates to #Believe. #Believe isn't a marketing slogan for me. It's who I am. You need to find who you are.

Then you can start making some important decisions.

HOW TO MAKE DECISIONS EASILY

> When your values are clear to you, making decisions
> becomes easier.
> —*Roy E. Disney (longtime senior executive at the Walt Disney Company,*
> *founded by his father, Roy, and uncle, Walt Disney)*

Making decisions can be hard . . .

. . . when you don't know what you stand for. Your One Word is your core. It's your guiding light. It makes all decisions easier. If you don't have that guiding light, then you never completely feel like you're going in the right direction. You'll constantly second-guess yourself, not being sure if you made the best choice. You'll spend more time agonizing over decisions than acting, than making a decision to improve your life and the lives of others.

When you know your One Word, you can make decisions that support your path.

Decisions that were difficult before now become easy to make. You know if you should start that business or not. You know if you should move to that city or not. You know if you should marry that person or not. It's also easy for people to understand who you are and how they can help you. Everything becomes easier. Your life, your business—everything becomes much easier.

It will also help you stay motivated.

HOW TO STAY MOTIVATED

> When you look at people who are successful, you will find that they aren't the people who are motivated, but have consistency in their motivation.
>
> —Arsène Wenger (French soccer manager and former player credited with revolutionizing soccer in England in the late 1990s)

Being an entrepreneur sucks a lot of the time.

It's hard to stay motivated. You might have a fantastic day, be on top of the world, and then the next morning wake up and find you're starting from scratch. You're doing something different, something new, something powerful, and it takes time to make it happen. You might have a #LittleMan in your life telling you all the reasons why you're not going to be successful. You might not be seeing any growth or momentum as you struggle to find your way. You might even be thinking of going back to get a job and do the "safe thing" to support your family. Man, it's hard staying motivated as an entrepreneur.

But you know what helps?

Feeling like you're doing something important. That's what people really want out of life.

That's probably what you hated about your last job. You wanted to wake up and feel like the work you were doing was important. When you get that feeling you're more likely to stay motivated. And that comes from finding your One Word and applying it to make a positive impact on the world.

People will also catch that motivation and help spread the word for you.

GETTING WORD OF MOUTH

If you do build a great experience, customers tell each other about that. Word of mouth is very powerful.

—*Jeff Bezos (billionaire cofounder of Amazon.com)*

If you don't get positive word of mouth, you're sunk.

You don't have the big budgets to take out a Super Bowl commercial or hire a celebrity spokesperson. You need people talking about you. Having a great product or service isn't enough. **You need to make it easy for people to talk about you.**

Think about how busy your customers are. They have opportunities every single day to promote you to their colleagues and friends. Every. Single. Day. And they don't. Why? It's not because they don't love your product or service. (If they don't, then you need to get to work at improving your offering!) **It's because you don't stand out enough.** They forget about you. You're just okay.

But when you stand for something important, something people feel connected to, something people are proud to be a part of, and you make it easy for them to share because they only have to re-member One Word, then referrals start to flow.

Make your message difficult, boring, and unremarkable and nobody will talk about you.

Make your message One Word, powerful, and important and people will be delighted to spread your message at every possible opportunity.

HOW TO #DELIGHT CUSTOMERS

> My goal is to delight my own family of customers, just like my dad did for his.
>
> —Louis Trahan (founder of Last Minute Training)

Louis Trahan had a problem—he's in a boring industry.

Louis's company, Last Minute Training, sells training for office workers. Most people don't think about training until they need it, and it's really hard to get people excited and talking about it. Most people see training as a necessary evil, not something to look forward to. When was the last time you went around telling everyone you know about the amazing Excel training you just can't wait to take?

Exactly.

But with my help, Louis realized that he doesn't *really* sell training. He sells the experience of being delighted. His One Word is #Delight and he built his entire business around it.

He delights his customers by actually caring about them. He and his team research and know more about all the training op-tions available than any other competitor so he can give the best recommendations to his clients.

He knows which training providers deliver the highest quality training for each subject area, who is least likely to cancel classes, and who has the best learning environment for his customers.

He often books people into courses where he makes less money because it's the right thing for the client.

When he interviews new staff members, he first looks at whether they have an attitude of delighting people before he looks at their skills, experience, or references.

In his marketing, he shows a picture of his baby son smiling because he wants people to feel delighted when they see his ads.

The results?

When I first met Louis and he joined my mastermind group, he had just an idea on paper. It was a pure start-up. Fast-forward a few years and Louis now has an office, a team, brand-name clients, sells over ten thousand training classes, and has booked almost $10 million in business. He's making money and making an impact.

So I asked Louis to share how he found his One Word.

LOUIS TRAHAN, MR. #DELIGHT

It wouldn't matter what kind of business I'm in, my number-one priority would still be to delight my customers.

—Louis Trahan (founder of Last Minute Training)

It was over twenty years ago—but I can still remember it like it was yesterday.

I woke up on Christmas morning, wondering where Dad was.

He was gone because it was cold outside. I mean REALLY cold outside (like fifty below) . . . and another family needed him to come fix their broken furnace.

He was a furnace repair man and these were his customers! Dad always went above and beyond to help a customer, even if they were total strangers. Especially on Christmas.

That wasn't the first (or last!) holiday without him. Dad hated seeing people suffering. I could tell you story after story where he aimed to bring joy and relief to the people around him, in every moment. Often at his own expense, or his family's.

And now I understand. We were ALL family to him. Every person.

Now my goal is to delight my own family of customers, just like my dad did for his. I can't help it; it's ingrained in me; it's part of my DNA.

And let's be honest, you probably rarely think of scheduling training as a delightful experience. In reality, it's probably a huge headache.

Most of our clients tell us they would previously spend hours AND HOURS researching, and then booking and managing multiple vendors for a variety of different training classes, only to get inadequate and even canceled classes!

We screen the vendors and trainers for quality, making sure we understand your needs to get you the right training, plus we negotiate the deal for you.

Our staff can often find you the right training class in minutes, when it might take you days to complete the search for the right class on your own.

I've built an entire team, made up of people who, just like my dad, will bend over backwards to delight you.

It wouldn't matter what kind of business I'm in, my number-one priority would still be to delight my customers.

It works for Louis and can work for any company. Honest!

THE #HONEST CO. STEPS UP

Everyone I approached was skeptical . . . Even my husband, Cash,
thought the idea was too big.

—Jessica Alba (cofounder of the Honest Company)

The Honest Company took its One Word to the next level.

Not only did cofounders Jessica Alba and Christopher Gavigan embrace the One Word philosophy, they named their business after their One Word, #Honest.

Jessica and Christopher were disgusted by how unhealthy
many children's products are. They are laced with toxic chemicals
that haven't been properly tested. They were making kids (and
Jessica) sick. She and Christopher got fed up.

**So they decided to be the change they wanted to see in the
world.**

They launched the Honest Company to provide nontoxic, eco-
friendly, fashionable, and affordable products for kids, ranging
from diapers to bath and body products.

They believed in their business so much that they hired Jessica's
mom to work for them. They love their manifesto and products so
deeply that they hang them on their wall.

Jessica practices #Honest management and the actress-
entrepreneur worth over $200 million doesn't have her own of-
fice. She sits right alongside her team.

They don't test their products on animals, they test them on
their own children. They give 1 percent of their revenue to charity
and chemical research.

From their employees to their suppliers, they think about the
impact they're leaving on the world. To reduce their carbon foot-
print everything they make is produced within 150 miles of Los
Angeles and they ship ground, not air.

They have unapologetically high standards in products, people, and business practices. Everything they do has to match up with their #Honest philosophy.

The results?

The Honest Company went from zero to hundreds of millions of dollars in sales. After three years in business, the company was valued at one billion dollars.

They are making money and making an impact by following their One Word.

So I asked Christopher to share his One Word story.

CHRISTOPHER GAVIGAN, MR. #HONEST

In our core mission, we don't talk about product. We talk about what's the change in the world we want to see and how do we accomplish that.

—*Christopher Gavigan (cofounder of the Honest Company)*

Early in my career, I was frustrated. I was frustrated with the lack of authentic relationships in business.

I was frustrated when I saw that everyone would promise you the world and then there was no consistent follow-up. That's being totally dishonest. What I found was the levels of transparency and authenticity and clarity and willingness to tell the consumer what was healthy and safe weren't there. And I'm thinking, "Wow, these are products that we're using on our bodies, in our homes, on our children, we're ingesting them . . . How is that possible?"

When my business partner, Jessica, and I were developing our concept we were imaging the world, dreaming big, and what we wanted in it. We were thinking about "What's the world we wanted?" I loved the beauty of the word "honest," the simplicity.

To be honest is something that everyone wants to be. It's an aspiration as well as a real-life fulfillment. It's an honor to hold that word. It's a privilege. And it's a duty. It holds you to a standard and it drives us forward every single day.

I wanted to challenge ourselves. To be honest, what does that mean? That's a lot to live up to. I wanted to see if we could do it. We're constantly, as a brand and as a company, pushing ourselves to really achieve, to be more and more honest every single day. Everyone is here to see this mission and purpose-driven company fulfill its core goal, and a lot of it is we're not here to build product. We're here to educate a new generation of consumers and parents. In our core mission, we don't talk about product. We talk about what's the change in the world we want to see and how do we accomplish that.

You have to align yourself with what you believe is right. What I love about us is we really act from our heart and if it doesn't feel right, we're not going to go there.

Honesty is telling people the truth even though it might be uncomfortable. It's quality. It's saying things that matter. It's telling people what you won't do and what's not inside as opposed to what is inside. We're everything from a baby diaper to shampoo to fruit and veggie washes to a range of lifestyle products. At the end of the day, a parent just wants to trust you. I guard that trust. I safeguard it every single day. It's the only thing we have, our credibility and trust. I am such a strong, passionate advocate of keeping that trust and that level of connectivity with that consumer and letting them know we are doing everything possible, every single day, to build and improve on that level of trust and connected relationship.

CHAPTER 2 HIGHLIGHTS

IMPORTANT TAKEAWAYS

- You can go as far as the mind lets you.
- *Gnothi seauton* = ancient Greek proverb used as a warning to pay no attention to the opinion of the masses.
- Marketing is about values. Apple's core value is that it believes it can change the world for the better.
- If you want to model Apple's amazing results, you need to get just as clear about who you are and what you stand for.
- Once you have clarity, everything else falls into place.
- If you're struggling to make a decision, sleep on it and see how you feel in the morning.
- Your One Word is more than a marketing slogan. It's a way of life.
- When you know your One Word, you can make decisions that support your path.
- What helps you stay motivated? Feeling like you're doing something important.
- Your One Word makes it easy for people to talk about you.
- The One Word philosophy has helped entrepreneurs generate millions in sales, and it can work for you too.

COMING UP: *In chapter 3, I'll show you how you can find your One Word.*

FINDING YOUR ONE WORD

People need to understand *that they have all the tools within themselves.*

—Deepak Chopra (bestselling author and a
  pioneer in the holistic health movement)

YOUR ONE WORD

Take five minutes to center yourself . . . if you don't have five
minutes, you don't deserve to have the life of your dreams.

—Oprah Winfrey (billionaire entrepreneur and creator of
  The Oprah Winfrey Show)

This is important.

The process you're about to go through is important.

It's one of the most valuable exercises you'll ever do in your life.

The results are life changing.

We're going to go over the Five Core Questions :

1. What makes you happy?
2. What connects your happiness?
3. What trait do you hate?
4. What's your constant?
5. Is this *really* who you are?

And then we'll discuss the Four Limiting Beliefs that hold you back from doing something great:

1. It's too bold.
2. What do you think?
3. Someone else is doing it.
4. It's too simple.

Have an open mind, be honest with yourself, and eliminate all distractions for the next thirty minutes.

Let's go!

1. WHAT MAKES YOU HAPPY?

I believe in pink. I believe that laughing is the best calorie burner. I believe in kissing, kissing a lot. I believe in being strong when everything seems to be going wrong. I believe that happy girls are the prettiest girls. I believe that tomorrow is another day and I believe in miracles.

—Audrey Hepburn (one of the greatest screen actresses of all time)

If you want to achieve success, start with what makes you happy.

Before worrying about what your One Word is, think about everything that makes you happy.

Start by making a list.

Just write what comes to mind and don't worry yet about where it leads you.

Get lost in happiness as you make your list.

Here are a few questions to get you started:

- What is your favorite movie?
- What is your favorite book?
- What is your favorite song?
- Who is your best friend?
- What is your favorite quote to live by?
- What kind of people do you like to hang out with?
- Who was your favorite boss?
- Why are you with your significant other?
- Who was your favorite teacher?
- What do/did you love most about your parents?
- What activities make you come alive?
- What do you look forward to most in your week?
- When was the last time you felt overwhelmingly happy?

These are all primers to get you thinking and writing.

Answer these questions and add whatever else comes to mind that makes you happy.

Fill the page with happiness and feel the energy that comes from it. It could be the path to your next half million dollars.

THE $500,000 #FAMILY

It's not about skill level—for the most part it's about an eagerness to help others, to be loving and make others feel comfortable, like family.

—*Sharon Galor (founder of Toronto Dance Salsa)*

When Sharon first walked into a salsa club and took to the floor, she was terrible.

She was so bad that one of the guys who asked her to dance left her in the middle of a song. And while that hurt, it didn't matter.

Despite her limited dancing abilities, she felt at home there because she loved the people. After only a week of dancing, she had a group of new friends and instantly felt like she belonged.

She had fallen in love with salsa and its community.

Meanwhile, she was on the fast track to success in her corporate-HR career. She had been promoted every year for five years in a row, was making a fantastic salary, and was considered to be a rising star at her company. But staying up until three every night dancing and waking up early to go to her real job was taking its toll.

Then she was forced to make an impossible decision.

Going out to practice every night made her a better dancer. Pretty soon the owner of a local ballroom-dance school asked her to teach for him, and then she spun off her salsa classes as her own business. Suddenly what she was doing for fun could be a full-time opportunity, but it would mean giving up her blossoming HR career.

She made the decision with her heart and knew she would never be as happy as when she was dancing. She gave up her job to launch Toronto Dance Salsa (TDS), willing to live on a much smaller salary if it meant she'd be happy. She never anticipated that she'd go from teaching a few classes a week to building a half-million-dollar business with multiple locations. She simply set out to create a place where everyone is included in the fun and where everyone feels at home.

Like family.

And that's why her family has grown to almost six thousand students learning salsa each year, making TDS one of the largest salsa studios in North America. TDS makes everyone feel a part of the family, with birthday dances for students and outings to salsa clubs. They have Helpers who are excited to volunteer their time so students get hands-on feedback. Helpers and staff alike are brought on based on whether they embody #Family, which is more important to Sharon than talent. Her students feel loved and welcomed, no matter their skill. Just like she felt when she started.

#Family is what made Sharon happy and what connects everything together for her growing business.

2. WHAT CONNECTS YOUR HAPPINESS?

Everything you do is connected to who you are as a person and, in turn, creates the person you are becoming.

—Paul E. Miller (author known for his books on spirituality)

This is where the magic starts to happen.

You have your page of all the things that make you happy, right?

(If not, do it now. It's important. Don't just read another book . . . I want you to take action.)

There is one common theme that connects all the things that make you happy.

You might have many reasons why Mrs. Jones was your favorite teacher.

There could be ten things you love about your favorite movie.

The people you hang out with have lots of different personalities.

But there is one theme that unites them all. One thing they, together, share. This is the connective tissue that will make all your future decisions easier.

This is the powerful mantra that will give you a sense of purpose and help you change the world for the better.

This is your One Word.

Find the common theme in the list of things that makes you happy, and write it down.

If it doesn't pop off the page, then next to each of the things that makes you happy write why you like it.

You'll notice a pattern that emerges: some words will come up over and over again. Take the words you've used most commonly to describe your happiest moments and group them together.

If you can't get it down to One Word yet, don't worry, just try to get the final list from this exercise down to five words or fewer.

Now we can take the next step in building your extraordinary life and business.

THE #EXTRAORDINARY WAY TO $1,000,000

If I'm able to live an extraordinary life, if I'm able to do extraordinary things, there's a gift in that. If I'm an extraordinary father, that's a gift for my kids. If I'm able to run an extraordinary business with extraordinary people, that's a culture that I'm able to give my staff.
—*Mark Drager (CEO of Phanta Media)*

Mark Drager didn't want to be ordinary.

After being an entrepreneur for a few years, he found himself feeling more and more like he wasn't making a significant contribution to his video-production company, Phanta Media. He had grown his business, hired people to do most of the tasks that he used to do, but he wanted to do something meaningful.

Mark felt lost.

After about six months of thinking about his role, he realized that his motivation didn't come from money. It never did. The prospect of making more money wouldn't push him to work harder. His motivation comes from recognition by others. He wants to stand out. He realized that had a deep fear of being ordinary—in all areas of his life.

Mark wanted to be extraordinary.

He wanted to be an extraordinary husband, an extraordinary father to his four kids, an extraordinary man of faith, an extraordinary member of his community, and an extraordinary entrepreneur.

When he was doing something extraordinary, it made him happy. That was the connective tissue for him. It was missing in his business, which made him feel lost, and for him to be happy and successful he knew he had to build his business around being extraordinary.

So he changed his company's mission to creating #Extraordinary video and aligned his entire business around it. He hires #Extraordinary staff members. He works on #Extraordinary projects. He creates #Extraordinary results for his clients. And his team holds him accountable as well to make sure everyone is giving an #Extraordinary effort. We'll go into his story in more detail in part 3 of this book.

Focusing on being #Extraordinary helped Mark pass his million-dollar revenue goal, and now he's going for more.

Finding his One Word wasn't something that came easily, but by digging deeper into who he was it became clear to him, and it can become clear to you as well.

DIG DEEPER TO FIND YOURSELF

If you cannot find peace within yourself, you will never find it anywhere else.

—Marvin Gaye (soul singer, songwriter, and musician who helped to shape the sound of Motown in the 1960s)

Now we're making progress!

Some people get their One Word immediately after step 2. They have their One Word and they're ready to apply it. If that's you, congrats!

For most people, the process is long and requires digging deeper. It was for me.

You may have written down multiple words and still feel unsure how to narrow them down to just one.

Does it have to be a verb? Can it be a noun? How about an adjective? The answer is, any of them. Verbs are often the easiest because they are action oriented. You might want to #Inspire the world or make an #Impact or #Contribute or #Shine or #Love.

But it doesn't have to be a verb.

For example, maybe your hero is your grandmother Jane, so you try to live a life inspired by her. #Jane becomes your One Word.

Or maybe you're like Audrey Hepburn and you "believe in pink." You get to define what #Pink means to you.

You can also combine multiple words that may seem like they're not related into a more meaningful One Word that unites them. For example if you love adventure but also value caring for others, maybe your One Word becomes #Heart, which you define as following your heart (adventure) and being heartfelt toward others (caring). You take two seemingly unrelated words and bring them together to form your One Word, like #Heart, to better define who you are and what kind of life you want to live.

This is a process.

You may have picked a word but you're not confident that it's right. You may feel that what you chose is too big, too daunting, too scary. If that's you, keep reading.

We'll figure it out together.

3. WHAT TRAIT DO YOU HATE?

The opposite of anger is not calmness, its empathy.

—*Mehmet Oz (cardiothoracic surgeon, author, and television personality better known as Dr. Oz)*

If you don't know who you are, then start by thinking of who you aren't.

Going negative helps a lot of people clarify their search for their One Word.

Think of all the things that make you unhappy and make a new list.

Write down the people you can't stand being around, the tasks you hate doing, the movies you never want to see, the things that make you dread going to work.

Make a list of everything and everyone that makes you unhappy.

Make it real.

Make it painful.

Nobody is judging you here.

If you can't stand the thought of seeing Aunt Suzie at Christmas, put her on the list.

But be careful.

This is not a list of your fears or your limiting personal beliefs.

It's a list of the traits that you truly are allergic to, that just bring you down, and that make you unhappy. The list is the start, but the power is in seeing what connects them.

Aunt Suzie, the boss you hated most, the people you despise being around, the tasks you dread doing—they too are all connected.

What theme binds them together?

When you've got it, think about the opposite to find your One Word.

For example if your negative theme is neglect, your One Word might be "care." If it's discourage, your One Word might be "inspire." Destroy turns into "create." Hate turns into "love," and so on.

It's time to turn your suffering into #Joy.

$5,000,000 WORTH OF #JOY

The reason why I got into this, and the reason why we attract the people and customers that we do, is because of this laser-beam focus on creating joy for the people we serve through the software we design. When we crystallized around that "why" and that One Word, magical things began to happen.

—*Richard Sheridan (cofounder of Menlo Innovations)*

Does work have to suck?

When Richard Sheridan started his multimillion-dollar custom-software development company, Menlo Innovations, he had a mission of "ending human suffering in the world as it relates to technology."

Richard understood that being a computer programmer could be frustrating, isolating, and miserable.

It was known as a "death march" when programmers pulled frequent all-nighters, postponed vacations, and put their personal lives aside for a project that often got dropped after months of hard work.

Richard knew there was a better way to run a company.

He wanted it to be a place where people would feel excited to come to work. But he realized that he couldn't focus on "not being a place of suffering."

He wanted to find a better way to describe the mission of his dream company.

Richard thought back to his childhood, when he had built a bookshelf for his parents, and to when he'd first laid his hands on a computer and wrote a miniprogram.

He got so much joy from building something that delighted others.

He also understood that an engineer simply wants to hear "I love what you designed, you made my life better." Likewise, he wanted to create joy for the people who use the software they'd design, which, in turn, would bring joy to those who created it!

Richard found his One Word, the opposite of the suffering he wanted to end: #Joy.

Since 2001, Menlo's mission has been to return #Joy to software development. They've grown to over five million dollars in revenue. Every business decision is easier with a clear mission: #Joy. And they've consistently been recognized for the culture of #Joy that they have fostered with their team, clients, and community. We'll dive deeper into his story in part 3 of this book.

Richard also realized that #Joy wasn't something he just discovered. It's something that, from childhood, has been a constant source of happiness for him.

4. WHAT'S YOUR CONSTANT?

I have always believed, and I still believe, that whatever good or bad fortune may come our way we can always give it meaning and transform it into something of value.

—Hermann Hesse (poet, novelist, and painter who, in 1946, received the Nobel Prize in Literature)

Your One Word is not a New Year's resolution.

This is not deciding on a word because you were inspired by a speech that you heard or seminar you attended.

It's not picking a word to be the person your parents or friends want you to be.

Your One Word is a constant.

It has always been with you and will always remain.

It's who you are and always have been.

Think about your favorite movie from ten years ago or from when you were a little child. You'll still like that movie today. You'll still like it in twenty years even though the special effects don't seem as great and the technology is dated. Because that movie means something to you. It represents a theme that is at the core of who you are.

So is your One Word.

Your One Word isn't something you get bored of or grow tired of.

It's always there and always will be.

If you're still trying to decide what your One Word is, look at your list of things that make you happy (from step 1) and think back to ten years ago.

What word best describes who you were back then?

Think about how you imagine your life in twenty years.

What word best describes who you'll be then?

Many things will change with time—your opinions, your environment, your family, your friends . . .

But your core value, your One Word, doesn't change.

You might want to start this process by looking to your parents.

ARE YOU LIKE YOUR PARENTS?

> They really just taught me at an early age the values of hard
> work. Both my parents are two of the hardest working people
> that I know, so that was a big foundation for me and something I
> really cherish and it really helped me to grow up in that kind of
> household.
>
> —*Blake Griffin (NBA All-Star basketball player known for*
>   *his hard work)*

If you're still having a hard time finding your constant, think back to your parents.

There's a reason psychologists ask their patients to talk about their relationship with their parents. Now, I'm no psychologist but I have found fairly consistently that someone's One Word often has roots back in their childhood and with their parents.

Quite often the core values you have today come from your parents.

They shaped the way you see the world, how you should treat others, and what you consider good and bad behavior. I've already told you my story about how my parents #Believed in me, told me that I was a Castrilli-Carmichael and I could achieve anything I put my mind to. I now pass that mindset on to my son. If your mother was caring, she might have taught you to care for others: #Care. If your father was resourceful, he might have instilled resourcefulness in you: #Resourceful.

The opposite can also be true.

> If I just do everything the opposite of what my dad did, I think that
> will make things pretty easy. I can joke about it now because I'm
> past that stage where it used to hurt. By having a kid, it's gone. I

could take all that negative energy that I had and put it in a positive way.

—*Derrick Rose (professional basketball player and youngest player ever to be selected NBA Most Valuable Player)*

You might have seen something in your parents that you *never* want to embody, so you take on the opposite of their values. If your mother had a gambling problem and constantly risked every paycheck she earned, you might seek to be the opposite of risk: #Security. If your father ran out on you when you were young and was never there for you growing up, you might crave to be the opposite of unreliable: #Dependable. They likely also transferred a lot of their limiting beliefs to you, and until you gain the awareness of them, you'll never break free (and you will likely continue the cycle with your own children—a topic for another book).

Spending a few minutes thinking about your parents and the mark they left on you could reveal the answer to finding your One Word.

You can build a life and a business around #Security or #Dependable just as much as you can around #Believe, #Care, or #Resourceful. Your parents impacted you in positive and negative ways. Having an awareness of their impact can set you up for future success.

If you get it right, you might be on your way to the next billion-dollar idea.

THE $1 BILLION #EMPATHY BUSINESS

To me it's about a focus on "them"—and by "them" I mean your employees and customers—as opposed to a focus on yourself. If you focus on "them" and their interests, good things happen to you as well.

—*Dheeraj Pandey (founder of Nutanix)*

Can you build a billion-dollar business by focusing on empathy?

Nutanix founder Dheeraj Pandey says yes.

Dheeraj grew up in India, and his lower-middle-class father insisted on giving to street beggars while most people would just walk past them. His mother also taught him that the process of giving to others makes you happy and good comes back to you. They ingrained in him the importance of being polite, sharing, and caring for others in everything he did.

They taught him to be empathetic with others.

So when Dheeraj came to America and started his enterprise-infrastructure company, he applied the foundational lessons from his parents and focused on feeling empathy for the needs and interests of his staff, clients, and partners.

Dheeraj understood that this wasn't all selfless: he knew it would be good for the company too. Like his mother explained, giving would make him happy and good would come back to him.

He saw that focusing on #Empathy would lead to success.

So he extended empathy first to his team—so much so that he shows immense trust by not bean counting their vacations, by helping with their education, and by paying 100 percent of their health care.

He also applied this to his customers. He designs products suited to what they really want, in ways that make it simple for them and give them peace of mind.

If they truly care about the customer "rather than geek out with a bunch of code or a bunch of fancy features," he explains, it will benefit everyone. They must think about the product through the customer's eyes. He sees this as the most natural way to develop a product.

He walks away from anyone who's in it for themselves. If he hears "I" too much in a conversation, he walks. He demands the same respect he gives and won't move forward unless there is a fair exchange of empathy. He doesn't sell a box. He sells an #Empathy experience.

#Empathy helped him build a billion-dollar business because it is a natural outlook for him. It's also one of the more popular One Words people use.

POPULAR ONE WORD EXAMPLES

> Thinking good thoughts is not enough, doing good deeds is not enough, seeing others follow your good examples is enough.
> —Douglas Horton (*Protestant clergyman and academic leader*)

Sometimes, in looking to set your path, it helps to see examples of what others are doing.

Below is a list of some of the most common One Words people have chosen by going through these exercises.

But first a quick disclaimer . . .

Don't feel restricted to having to use any of these words. Just because others are using them it doesn't mean you should or shouldn't. Let the list act as a spark of inspiration to get your creativity flowing.

Here are some of the more popular One Word options people have chosen:

#Action	#Battle	#Commit
#Adapt	#Be	#Confidence
#Adventure	#Brave	#Courage
#Ambition	#Celebrate	#Curious
#Balance	#Change	#Dare

#Determined	#Love	#Relentless
#Direction	#Mindfulness	#Resolve
#Discover	#Minimize	#Revel
#Empathy	#Momentum	#Risk
#Empower	#Open	#Shine
#Finish	#Opportunity	#Silence
#Focus	#Optimism	#Simplify
#Fortitude	#Organize	#Soar
#Freedom	#Peace	#Strength
#Grace	#Persistence	#Thrive
#Growth	#Possibility	#Together
#Ignite	#Present	#Transformation
#Imagine	#Purpose	#Transition
#Invest	#Rebuilding	#Unstoppable
#Learn	#Reduce	#Uplift
#Listen	#Reflection	

You don't have to pick from this list. Just make sure to go with what's in your heart—and the answer is definitely not #Money.

MY ONE WORD IS "MONEY"

Money has never made man happy, nor will it, there is nothing in its nature to produce happiness."
—*Benjamin Franklin (one of the Founding Fathers of the United States and renowned statesman)*

What, you might ask, if my One Word is "money"?
It's not. If you think it is, you just haven't found what truly

makes you come alive. Now, don't get me wrong, money is great. Money lets us do amazing things. We need to make money to stay alive, and the more money we make, the more we can build.

But understand this: money is a tool, not a core value.

It can help take you where you want to go, but it's not the driver. There is always something deeper behind the need for money, and until you figure that out, you'll always limit yourself. Money comes from providing value. If people aren't willing to pay you for what you're doing, you're not giving them enough value. On the flip side, the way to make a lot of money quickly is to provide a lot of value quickly.

Why do you love money so much?

Say your dream is to make enough money in the next year to travel around the world. What you're really seeking isn't money; it's #Adventure, #Experiences, or #Excitement. What most people do is set a money goal, then try to figure out the fastest way to reach that money goal. They take on a business opportunity that they aren't excited about because it promises to move them closer to their money goal. They tell themselves they don't care what they do (within reason) as long as it brings in the money, because that's their real goal. They say it doesn't matter.

But it does matter.

Money comes from giving value, and if you don't have the love for your business, then you won't put in the crazy work that's needed to provide that value. You'll quit as soon as it starts getting hard. And the idea of working hard at something you don't like just so you can live the life you want at some point in the future is crazy to me. Start living that life now. Let's go back to our example of wanting money to travel but the real driver is #Adventure, #Experiences, or #Excitement. Well, build #Adventure, #Experiences, and #Excitement into your business right now! Start a business where you get to travel right now. Do what you've always wanted to do right now—and stop waiting. You're also way more likely to be successful because you're enjoying the process of doing the work and not just seeking the end result.

Saying that money is your One Word is a crutch. You just haven't dug deep enough inside yourself to discover who you really are.

5. IS THIS *REALLY* WHO YOU ARE?

People have to learn who they are—you can't have somebody else telling you who you are.

—*Hale Irwin (one of the world's leading golfers from the mid-1970s to the mid-1980s)*

For all of this to work, you have to be brutally honest and real with yourself.

This isn't about who you "should be" or hope to be.

It's not about what your family wants you to be or what your culture tells you to be.

It's about who you really are, and leveraging that to build a purposeful and happy life for yourself.

It's about living your version of your life and following your dream, not theirs.

If you keep living in a world where you can't be yourself and you're constantly striving for this ideal life of someone who isn't who you actually are, you'll never be fulfilled.

You don't have to be ashamed or afraid of your One Word.

It's who you are and it will guide you for the rest of your life.

Look at your One Word and ask yourself, "Is this really, deep down, who I am?"

If you answer yes, you're ready to move on to build something #Awesome.

(If you answer no, go back and try the exercises again. Sleep on it. Reflect on it in the shower. Go for a walk and think about it. Meditate on it. And if you still don't know, reach out to me and we can try to set up a session to go over it).

THE FULL-TIME #AWESOME BUSINESS

It's irrelevant whether you see [the glass] as half full or half empty. Take the opportunity to just fill it—create that value, fill that void.

—*Roberto Blake (graphic designer, speaker, educator, and marketer)*

Roberto Blake has done something that many people are jealous of.

He has built a full-time income for himself as a graphic designer and marketer by focusing on what was real to him—doing things that are #Awesome.

Roberto used to be like most people. He always wanted to create his dream business but never seemed to move forward with it. He wanted to write a book, start a YouTube channel, get into podcasting, and so much more . . . But life just seemed to always get in the way.

He'd been aware of his desire to create #Awesome for many years. He had a successful design and marketing company, but he had bigger plans.

Roberto kept telling himself that "maybe someday" he'd get to it—until one man forced him to.

That man was a mugger who robbed him outside a bar. That blood-pumping experience put everything into perspective for Roberto. He realized that the outcome could have very easily been very different and it was time to make some important decisions.

He asked himself, what would he want to do if he were locked in a room for all eternity? His answer was that he wanted to create #Awesome things, share them with the world, and teach other people how to do the same.

It was time to do a self-audit and examine how he was spending his time. He had to change his schedule to fit his priorities.

Roberto went all in to create #Awesome.

He's dedicated to being a leader for other people like him—artists, musicians, writers, anyone who wants to create things and bring them into the world. He mentors others by pouring his time into offering feedback on their work, videos, and social media.

When you get real with yourself and make your dreams a priority, you can create something #Awesome too, as long as you believe you can.

THE FOUR LIMITING BELIEFS

Whether you think you can or you think you can't—you're right.

—*Henry Ford (founder of the Ford Motor Company)*

You are where you are because of what you believe.

You are a product of your environment, the people around you, and the media and information that you consume.

There are Four Limiting Beliefs that hold you where you are. They are:

1. It's too bold.
2. What do you think?
3. Someone else is doing it.
4. It's too simple.

If you've ever had big goals but for some reason never took action . . .

If you've ever started something you really wanted to do and then stopped . . .

If you've ever built something to a certain level of success but then hit a plateau that you couldn't break through . . .

Chances are it's because of your limiting personal beliefs.

If you want to change your circumstances, you start by changing your beliefs.

Your One Word is a big deal.

It's the life-changing, world-impacting, history-writing kind of deal.

And chances are the limiting beliefs (we all have some) that have held you back from doing big things before will hold you back again this time around.

So we need to start by addressing the four most common limiting beliefs many people have about their One Word.

Let's go break some of your limiting beliefs!

1. IT'S TOO BOLD

Our deepest fear is not that we are inadequate. Our deepest fear is that we are powerful beyond measure. It is our light, not our darkness that most frightens us. We ask ourselves, Who am I to be brilliant, gorgeous, talented, and fabulous? Actually, who are you not to be? You are a child of God. Your playing small does not serve the world. There is nothing enlightened about shrinking so that other people will not feel insecure around you . . . It is not just in some of us; it is in everyone and as we let our own light shine, we unconsciously give others permission to do the same. As we are liberated from our own fear, our presence automatically liberates others.

—*Marianne Williamson (spiritual teacher, author, and lecturer)*

"It's too big, too daring, too bold."

"Who am I to have such a big word like that?"

Stop. Right. There.

The story you tell yourself about what you can't do has hurt you for your entire life.

Don't let it keep you down now. This is too important. Your One Word is *supposed* to be big. It's supposed to inspire and motivate you.

It's supposed to be bold.

Exercise 1: Think about yourself at age eighty, looking back on your life. Are you going to regret that you didn't take action and believe in yourself because you were scared?

Exercise 2: Reflect on the message you want to spread to your children and grandkids. How are you going to authentically encourage them to follow their dreams when you didn't follow yours?

Exercise 3: Look back on the first time you tried something new. You were scared and nervous. The next time it was easier—and even easier the time after that. Being bold becomes easier every time you practice being bold.

Exercise 4: Research the story of any famous entrepreneur you look up to. Chances are they started off in a situation that is no better than yours right now (it was probably way worse), and they made it. You can too.

Look at your One Word and feel empowered. Feel the energy that comes from it.

You're going to use it to do great things and impact the lives of many people.

Be bold, be proud, and love it.

CAN #LOVE MAKE YOU MILLIONS?

It really is about listening to your gut. If you're sitting in that room and people are looking at you like that, and every little microorganism in your stomach is saying "don't do it, don't do it," then it would be so inauthentic and wrong of me to say yes.

—*Maria Rodale (CEO of Rodale Publishing and Rodales.com)*

Maria was afraid to go public with the One Word that motivated her in business.

She's the leader behind the multimillion-dollar family-owned publishing institution Rodale Publishing, an independent company publishing some of the largest, most established health and wellness lifestyle brands, including *Men's Health*, *Women's Health*, and *Runner's World*, and is one of the largest independent book publishers in the United States. The company was started by her grandfather and was later taken over by her father, who tragically died in a car accident. After his death a friend asked her how she kept working there despite the trauma. At that moment she instinctively knew it was because she felt it was a spiritual mission of #Love.

#Love was her secret word.

She feels that #Love is the thread that unites people and connects everything in a beautiful way. Whenever she put her job into the context of finding what people love, she found it rewarding.

But she was tentative about sharing it with everyone at her company. She wasn't sure everyone would understand what #Love had to do with business.

Years after she took over the business, she heard Starbucks founder Howard Schultz speak, and he was asked about what really drives him. His answer? "Love." From that point on, Maria realized that she could admit her passion for the word too.

She felt such relief, knowing she too could be bold and talk about #Love in business.

Her company has transformed since she's boldly made decisions for the business around #Love. It shifted resources, attention, and energy away from old strategies that weren't working, and toward the new things focused on #Love.

Over the years, Maria observed that a book or magazine will usually perform better when a Rodale advocate is truly loving the project. Many projects require a long-term commitment, so they're stuck with it for a while. They have to love it to commit. At the end of the day, she knows they need to believe in their publications, and that's all about #Love.

Maria saw how the world is changing direction when it comes to business. She believes that people, now more than ever, want to buy from companies that have a sense of values, that care about each other and the earth.

Maria learned to confidently choose what she #Loves for her business and she no longer cares what others think about her One Word.

2. WHAT DO YOU THINK?

When you follow your heart, you're never supposed to do things because of what you think people might say. You do it for the opposite reasons.

—will.i.am (singer, songwriter, entrepreneur, actor, record producer, and philanthropist best known as a founding member of the Black Eyed Peas)

Stop being ruled by the opinions and judgments of other people.

It's okay to be collaborative. It's okay to seek people's counsel. It's okay to ask for guidance. But if you're unable to take action until you get the go-ahead from someone else, then you'll never truly be in control of your life.

As I coach people through this process, I often get asked, "Evan, from what you know of me, what do you think of my One Word?"

This is *your* life. Live it. You don't need anyone's permission.

Finding your One Word is a very personal and intimate experience. I recommend searching for it in isolation from others. It doesn't matter what your friends or family think. Don't ask for their approval. Instead, go deeper within yourself to find it.

Take a few long walks. Meditate. Go away. Disconnect. Sleep on it. Hike. Bike. Run. Shower. If your One Word doesn't come to you immediately, then you need to give yourself the mental space to figure it out.

Don't talk with others more. Talk with yourself more.

This is your purpose and only you get to decide. You need to stop living *their* version of your life and start living *your* version of your life.

Get to the point where you have your One Word and you feel so good about it that it doesn't matter who tells you it's wrong. You're sticking with it because it's who . . . you . . . are.

I can't pick your purpose.

I can't answer the question for you.

Nobody can.

I can be your coach, but I can't get on the field and score a touchdown for you. That's on you.

The last thing you want to do is make a big decision like this based on what other people are thinking instead of making your fantasy come true.

THE WORD THAT SELLS A #FANTASY

> In the process of writing it down, and being able to read the words, you can feel it and imagine it more, and it makes it real.
> —Jennifer Price (founder of Much, Inc.)

Jen loved to daydream.

At first it seemed silly to apply that in her copy-writing business. But as she thought about her passion for writing her clients' dreams into reality, she realized that #Fantasy was the key. She knew the truth: that writing a sales page for a new product actually means helping a customer feel their #Fantasy by showing them how the product helps them become who they want to be.

Logic doesn't make the sale. #Fantasy does.

Jen gets that the real power in a business plan isn't that it will be followed to the letter, but that it paints a picture that compels others, whereas a random unwritten idea will get zero momentum. Writing down a #Fantasy is the first step in making it come true.

She decided to pick a word that isn't easy for most to digest.

She could have chosen a more common word like "dream" or "imagine." But for her, #Fantasy was so much bigger than that. It included those concepts, but it also embodied her mission to help people find pleasure in their daily lives, to fearlessly embrace the things that they desire, and to share them with others so they have closer connections and gain allies for their #Fantasies.

People told her that #Fantasy didn't make sense for business.

She was told that #Fantasy had too many other connotations, like fantasy sports and fantasy sex, which could confuse potential clients. Even after she settled on #Fantasy, and included it in her branding, she was told by her own family that she should create a generic brand on the side—one that didn't include the word

#Fantasy. They meant well, but their advice came from fear of not being able to attract clients. Jen chose to listen to her heart, not let others' fears dictate her brand.

Not everyone is going to get it.

People will have different interpretations of your One Word, but when you tell your story and why you stand for it, you'll get clients who are a better fit. Jen attracts clients willing to pay a premium for #Fantasy because it's *not* generic copy they can get elsewhere. Jen's One Word makes her extra valuable and extra attractive.

Jen's clients connect with her One Word even if it has multiple meanings or someone else is using it.

3. SOMEONE ELSE IS DOING IT

> If I have seen further than others, it is by standing upon the shoulders of giants.
>
> —Isaac Newton (*English physicist and mathematician widely seen as one of the most influential scientists of all time*)

The more powerful a word you pick, the more it will have been used already.

My One Word, #Believe, has been used over and over and over again.

There have been seven movies and TV shows called *Believe*.

There are twenty-eight music albums called *Believe*. There are almost forty songs put out by major artists called "Believe."

Justin Bieber and Cher both had Believe music tours.

Britney Spears launched a fragrance line called Believe.

Believe was the name of one of Shamu the whale's shows at SeaWorld.

Believe was a marketing campaign used to promote the Halo 3 video game.

"Believe" has been used over and over again and will continue to be used because it's a powerful word with a lot of meaning.

So does that mean I can't use it?

Absolutely not.

I'm putting my own mark on the word. I'm using it in ways others haven't yet.

Remember: you get to assign your own meaning to the word.

#Believe for me means (1) having **passion** for what you're doing, (2) having **confidence** in yourself to start, and (3) having the **conviction** to follow through.

Everything I do embodies those three elements of #Believe.

So if someone has already "taken" your One Word, that's great!

It means it's powerful, and if you put your own twist on the word, you can have a big impact on the world.

The unique part isn't the word but, instead, your *take* on the word.

ARE YOU UNIQUE?

Today you are You! That is truer than true! There is no one alive who is Youer than You!

—Dr. Seuss (children's book author with over 600 million in book sales)

What do you do if someone is already using your One Word?

The Honest Company is a consumer-goods business, co-founded by activist Christopher Gavigan and actress Jessica Alba, that promotes nontoxic household products and ethical consumerism. They have a valuation of over $1 billion. We've already talked about them (more coming later on, as well). Because they embrace #Honest and put it in their name, does that mean other companies can't also be #Honest? Absolutely not. Here are two great examples.

Honest Tea

Honest Tea is a bottled organic-tea company based in Bethesda, Maryland. It was founded in 1998 by Seth Goldman and Barry Nalebuff. They wanted to create a tea that was honest to the original flavor. So they made sure it tasted like tea and wasn't oversweetened. They care for the earth and want to have a positive impact. Honest Tea uses only fair-trade organic tea leaves and even provided eye care for six thousand villagers living in a community that picks leaves for them so it would be easier to do their job. Seth and Barry also care deeply about building honest relationships. Before he launched the company, Seth took five thermoses of kitchen-brewed tea to a Whole Foods buyer to taste, before they were even manufacturing it. Whole Foods became his first partner, and they maintain this partnership today. Coca-Cola purchased a 40 percent stake in the company for $43 million in 2008 and bought the rest of the company in 2011. The 2015 sales were projected to be around $178 million.

*Honest Agency

*Honest Agency is a creative agency based in Winnipeg, Manitoba, that provides branding, design, strategy, advertising, web design, and public relations, and was cofounded by Callum Beattie and Sherril Matthes. They have ten employees, are close to $1 million in sales, and work with brand-name clients in their region. They added the asterisk to their name, which serves as a footnote that they are honest in all their practices, but also as a little joke on how the advertising industry uses disclaimers to qualify claims as true. They encourage customers to be honest about themselves and to move forward as a stronger, more authentic brand, and because of their own brand, they attract clients who are socially responsible, and they help them tell their story.

#Honest is simple, meaningful, and each entrepreneur has put his or her own take on it.

4. IT'S TOO SIMPLE

Life is really simple, but we insist on making it complicated.

—*Confucius (philosopher and founder of Confucianism)*

It's too simple.

"I can't be put into one single word. I want to say more." This is a common reaction from people when they look at their One Word.

If this is your reaction, then you probably needlessly overcomplicate a lot of things in your life or business.

Understand that there is incredible power and freedom in simplicity. Power to set the direction of, and change, your life. Power to make it easy for people to help you on your journey. Power to impact millions of people and change their lives.

Like Steve Jobs said, it's "about values. This is a very complicated world. It's a very noisy world. And we're not going to get a chance to get people to remember much about us . . . And so, we have to be really clear on what we want them to know about us."

Remember that you get to define what your One Word means to you.

Your One Word can represent parallel ideals that all have deep meaning.

Most people think #Believe is about believing in yourself (self-confidence). That's only part of what it means to me. To me it's also about believing in what you're doing (following your passion) and believing it will work out (perseverance). "Confidence," "passion," and "perseverance" are all related words brought together in my One Word, #Believe.

That's what turns "believe" into #Believe.

Recall the example from earlier to turn multiple words into One Word:

You can also combine multiple words that may seem like they're not related into a more meaningful One Word that unites them. For example if you love adventure but also value caring for others, maybe your One Word becomes #Heart, which you define to be following your heart (adventure) and being heartfelt toward others (caring). You take two unrelated words and bring them together to form your One Word, #Heart, to better define who you are and what kind of life you want to live.

With simplicity there is power, alignment, and purpose.
Get it down to One Word.

WINSTON CHURCHILL: VICTORY

Winston Churchill was the prime minister of the United Kingdom from 1940 to 1945 and again from 1951 to 1955. He is widely regarded as one of the greatest wartime leaders of the twentieth century. Churchill is the only British prime minister to have won the Nobel Prize in Literature since its inception in 1901, and he was the first person to be made an honorary citizen of the United States. Let's hear what he had to say about victory to a nation at war (emphasis mine):

> *All the great things are simple, and many can be expressed in a single word.*
>
> *I have nothing to offer but blood, toil, tears and sweat. We have before us an ordeal of the most grievous kind. We have before us many, many long months of struggle and of suffering. You ask,*

what is our policy? I can say: It is to wage war, by sea, land and air, with all our might and with all the strength that God can give us; to wage war against a monstrous tyranny, never surpassed in the dark, lamentable catalogue of human crime. That is our policy.

You ask, what is our aim? I can answer in one word: It is victory, victory at all costs, victory in spite of all terror, victory, however long and hard the road may be.

Never give in—never, never, never, never, in nothing great or small, large or petty, never give in except to convictions of honour and good sense. Never yield to force; never yield to the apparently overwhelming might of the enemy.

*If you will not fight for right when you can easily win without bloodshed; if you will not fight when your **victory** is sure and not too costly; you may come to the moment when you will have to fight with all the odds against you and only a precarious chance of survival. There may even be a worse case. You may have to fight when there is no hope of **victory**, because it is better to perish than to live as slaves.*

We shall not flag or fail. We shall go on to the end. We shall fight in France, we shall fight on the seas and the oceans, we shall fight with growing confidence and growing strength in the air, we shall defend our island, whatever the cost may be. We shall fight on the beaches, we shall fight on the landing grounds, we shall fight in the fields and in the streets, we shall fight in the hills; we shall never surrender.

*In war, resolution; in defeat, defiance; in **victory**, magnanimity.*

*God bless you all. This is your **victory**! It is the **victory** of the cause of freedom in every land. In all our long history we have never seen a greater day than this. Everyone, man or woman, has done their best. Everyone has tried. Neither the long years, nor the dangers, nor the fierce attacks of the enemy, have in any way weakened the unbending resolve of the British nation. God bless you all.*

CHAPTER 3 HIGHLIGHTS

IMPORTANT TAKEAWAYS

- People need to understand that they have all the tools within themselves.
- Finding your One Word is one of the most important exercises you will ever do in your life.
- If you want to succeed, then you need to start with what makes you happy.
- Find the common theme from the list of things that make you happy and write it down. This is where the magic starts to happen.
- If you don't know who you are, then start by thinking of who you aren't. Make a list of everything and everyone that makes you unhappy, and figure out what binds them together.
- Your One Word is not a New Year's resolution. It's a constant. It's not something you get bored of. Your core value, your One Word, doesn't change.
- For all of this to work, you have to be brutally honest and real with yourself. It's about living your version of your life and following your dream, not theirs.
- You are where you are because of what you believe. If you want to change your circumstances, you start by changing your beliefs.
- The story you tell yourself about what you can't do has hurt you for your entire life. Your One Word is supposed to be bold. Be bold, be proud, and love it.
- Don't talk more with others. Talk more with yourself. Stop being ruled by the opinions and judgments of other people. This is your life. Live it. You don't need anyone's permission.

- The more powerful a word you pick, the more it will have been used. The unique part isn't the word but, rather, your take on it.
- If "it's too simple" is your reaction, then you probably needlessly overcomplicate a lot of things in your life or business. Remember that you get to define what your One Word means to you. Get it down to One Word.

COMING UP: *In chapter 4, I'll show you how to build a movement around your One Word.*

CAMPAIGN

There are many elements to a campaign. Leadership is number one.
Everything else is number two.
—*Bertolt Brecht (poet, playwright, and theater director)*

IN PART 2: CAMPAIGN, you're ready to take your One Word and start to apply it to create a campaign for your business. *Something people will care about.* You'll learn how to get all the pieces in place to launch your campaign, and we will run through *a checklist* of everything you'll need to get started. You'll also find *case studies* and expertise culled from interviews with business leaders and an action plan modeled after my own *#Believe campaign.*

CHAPTER 4

BUILD A MOVEMENT

One individual can begin a movement
that turns the tide of history. Martin Luther
King in the civil rights movement, Mohandas
Gandhi in India, Nelson Mandela in South
Africa are examples of people standing up
with courage and non-violence to bring
about needed changes.

—*Jack Canfield (coauthor of the bestselling
Chicken Soup for the Soul series)*

CAN YOU CHANGE THE WORLD?

No matter what people tell you, words and ideas can
change the world.

—*Robin Williams (Academy Award–winning actor and comedian)*

This is where the real fun begins.

People are yearning so much to find meaning and purpose in
their lives that when you give them an opportunity to be a part of
something important, they jump on board.

It started with my sister.

I like to test things on a small scale before expanding.

Prove that it works before you go too far down the wrong path.

Testing on a small scale also lets you get started quickly.

You don't have to spend months planning—just find something easy and start!

The easiest thing for me to change was my newsletter.

So instead of writing my usual newsletters, I wrote a personal message to my subscribers talking about #Believe.

My sister Stefanie was one of the first to reply.

Her message: "I like your newsletters a lot more. I actually read them now!"

Thanks, Sis. I was off to a good start.

More people started to write in and my newsletter engagement jumped 50 percent.

The movement began with a simple test.

THE NO. 1 MARKETING SECRET: TEST

The most important word in the vocabulary of advertising is TEST. Test your promise. Test your media. Test your headlines and your illustrations. Test the size of your advertisements. Test your frequency. Test your level of expenditure. Test your commercials. Never stop testing, and your advertising will never stop improving.

—David Ogilvy (widely hailed as the Father of Advertising and called "the most sought-after wizard in today's advertising industry" by Time magazine)

One simple test changed my entire business.

After years of testing headlines and measuring copy and tracking clicks on links—you know, doing all the important marketing stuff everyone tells you to do . . .

The single biggest change I made, in terms of impact, was writing about my One Word, #Believe.

I spent so much time testing the wrong things and making

continuous but minor improvements that I missed testing the biggest thing of all: the core.

#Believe worked in my newsletter, so I expanded.

I redid my website.

I reworked my YouTube videos.

I changed my social media campaigns.

Everything became about #Believe.

And a movement took off.

People started hashtagging #Believe.

Others sent me pictures and songs that related to #Believe.

All of a sudden I had fans and they wanted #Believe T-shirts and hoodies.

Artists were contributing music, YouTube stars were making tribute videos, designers were creating #Believe graphics.

Anything I did around #Believe automatically took off faster than my older content.

It was clear. It was powerful. It meant something to people.

My tests created meaningful examples of how #Believe led to results.

THIS EXAMPLE SHOCKED ME

A person always doing his or her best becomes a natural leader, just by example.

—Joe DiMaggio (National Baseball Hall of Fame player)

This one example rocked my world.

It really made me see how powerful my One Word was and how much time I had wasted running in circles before. At the time of this test, I was all-in on YouTube. It was my favorite content platform, and I had thousands of videos on my YouTube channel.

The most popular one of all used to be me telling the story of Chris Gardner and how he went from being homeless to becoming a millionaire. It's the story that Will Smith took to Hollywood in the movie *The Pursuit of Happyness*. In one year my video got 105,000 views. Not bad, right? A lot of people would love to have 100K views on a single video. Heck, I was thrilled with the results!

My #Believe strategy was working on my newsletter, so I thought I'd expand it to my videos.

If it worked here, I'd go all-in on #Believe on YouTube too. The next video I released was called "BELIEVE," which embodied the foundational messages of passion, self-confidence, and conviction that made up #Believe for me. In less than a month it had over 150,000 views.

Wait . . . What???

I had 50 percent better results in one month than I'd had with my old video, which took an entire year to break the hundred-thousand-view barrier. I was onto something big here. Fast forward: the "BELIEVE" video now has over one million views.

Fast forward to today:

When you stand for something powerful, something that means something to you, something that other people can easily understand—people will share it. People will rally behind you. You'll be happier, have a greater impact, make more money, feel like you're contributing, have more energy—and you'll start to build a movement.

You can build your powerful movement by planning an effective campaign. In the next chapter, I'll outline the step-by-step process with which I built my movement, how other game changers built theirs, and how you can build yours.

But first let's address a very real issue that every entrepreneur faces at some point: staying motivated.

STAYING MOTIVATED

Whatever you do, don't ever use a crutch, and don't ever
think of having an excuse for not having said, "Yeah,
I did my best."

—*Isadore Sharp (founder of the Four Seasons
Hotels and Resorts)*

Give it your very best.

When people look back on their lives, they often wish they had taken more chances and had had the courage to believe in themselves a little more.

Finding your One Word is scary, overwhelming, and exhilarating all at once.

It can lead to some very deep and meaningful realizations about the kind of life you're living right now, and if it's a true reflection, of the life you want to live.

If you feel stuck where you are right now, it's likely because you are living out of alignment with what you should be doing. You're not living your One Word—and making the necessary decisions to change can be painful and daunting.

You might have so much invested in what you're currently doing. How can you change now? You've put so much money in. You've spent years of your life doing this. You've told your friends and the public. What would they think of you if you moved on to something completely different? Are you a complete failure?

I get it. The fear is real, as it should be. The answer isn't to be unafraid but rather to feel the fear and do it anyway because this is your only shot at living up to your true potential instead of continuing on in mediocrity.

You owe it to yourself to try so you don't have any regrets later in life.

You have to give it your very best. If you don't really give it your best shot, it's almost as bad as not trying at all.

You'll always wonder what could have happened if only you tried harder.

You'll forever live with the regret of not putting a serious effort into being who you are.

We rarely regret the things we try and fail at, and the upside is we get to live our dreams.

It's usually the things we don't really try that linger and haunt us for the rest of our lives.

Don't be that person.

If you take a giant swing, with all your effort, and miss, it'll hurt for a while, but you'll learn from it, and you'll pick yourself back up by finding a different way to stand. If you don't give it your very best, you'll always wish you had and wonder about the possibilities of what might have been.

Take your shot so you can start living large.

LIVING LARGE WITHOUT LIMBS

FAITH: Full Assurance In The Heart.

—*Nick Vujicic (evangelist and motivational speaker born without any of his four limbs)*

No arms. No legs. Could you keep your dreams alive?

Through #Faith, Nick Vujicic did.

Nick was born in Australia with a rare disease that left him without arms or legs. His parents soon got over their shock and were determined to help him enjoy life.

He was the first special-needs student in Australia integrated into the public education system, and he learned to swim, surf, and skateboard with his peers.

But Nick continued to get bullied and feel depressed.

At age ten, Nick tried to kill himself in a bathtub. But then he thought of his parents, and realized he didn't want to leave them with heartache or guilt. So he didn't go through with it, though he continued to struggle emotionally.

He didn't think he had anything to look forward to.

It wasn't until, at age thirteen, his attitude changed when he decided to put his #Faith in God, believing that there must be a reason why he was born without limbs.

One day his school's janitor heard his story of #Faith and encouraged him to share it with others. He nervously spoke to an auditorium full of tenth graders, many of whom were visibly moved to tears.

One girl asked if she could come up and hug him onstage, and thanked him for making her feel loved and beautiful.

He gave her #Faith, and her response inspired him to keep speaking.

Nick founded his nonprofit, Life Without Limbs, while still in school. He went on to college and got a degree in accounting and financial planning, and continued to practice his speaking skills. He later started his for-profit company, Attitude Is Altitude, also focused around speaking to inspire others.

He has since spoken to audiences over a thousand times, affecting over four million people in more than fifty countries with his message of #Faith, perseverance, and love. This led to a TED talk and, most recently, a podcast series that is reaching millions more.

Nick relentlessly encourages others to have #Faith and pursue their passions no matter what the circumstances: "If I can dream big, so can you."

Nick believes that you'll stay motivated when you find your true purpose.

3 STEPS TO MOTIVATION

We all have those things that even in the midst of stress and disarray, they energize us and give us renewed strength and purpose.

—Adam Braun (founder of Pencils of Promise)

If you're not motivated, you won't create great work.

It's easy to get caught up in the day-to-day grind of running a business. Sometimes you just don't feel like getting up and going to work. The following will help serve as a quick motivational tool whenever you feel like you're not giving it all you have.

Here are three things to think about to keep you motivated:

1. *What do you hate about being an employee?*

   Avoiding pain is often the biggest motivator to get people to take action. If you don't give it your best and get your company moving, what's going to happen? You'll end up having to go get a job again. It's time for having a bad boss, working to make someone else wealthy, not being challenged, having a terrible schedule, and not being paid what you're worth. Is that enough of a kick in the pants to get you working? Write down the five things you hate most about being an employee. You don't ever want to go back here! Make these as painful as possible!

2. *Why did you start?*

   If the stick didn't work, try the carrot. Why did you want to be an entrepreneur? What are you doing to help people through your business? What is your One Word and how are you able to leverage it to make a better life for you, your family, and the people around you? Write down five positive things that get you excited about your business. You can also include testimonials from happy clients if they are charged with emotion and make you feel good.

3. *What do you want to be remembered for?*

   Think about what you want to accomplish in life. What kind of impact do you want to have? Money is only a motivator for so long and won't buy you happiness. How do you want to be remembered? What do you want your grandkids to learn about you? Write down five things that you want to accomplish through your business. These should be aspirational and get you pumped up. Remember, none of these things will happen if you don't start giving your business 100 percent right now!

The next time you're feeling sluggish or down, refer to these points. If they don't kick you out of your funk, you need to work at them. Otherwise you'll quit and soon be back slaving away for someone else.

Another tactic I use is to look at motivational quotes from three of my heroes: Steve Jobs, Oprah Winfrey, and Tony Robbins.

MY FAV MOTIVATING QUOTES

> For quotes, I have one document for general quotes; the other
> for happiness-related quotes, which I use for the "Moment of
> Happiness," my daily emails of happiness quotes.
>
> —*Gretchen Rubin (bestselling author of* The Happiness
> Project, *blogger, and speaker)*

**Great quotes can inspire you to keep going and save you in
your darkest times.**

I made a list of quotes that inspire me. When I doubt myself or
think about quitting, I return to this list to keep me strong and to
fight another day.

STEVE JOBS

Believe that things will work out . . . follow your intuition and
curiosity . . . trust your heart even when it leads you off the well-
worn path . . . You have to trust that the dots will somehow connect
in your future . . . The only way to do great work is to love what you
do. If you haven't found it yet, keep looking. Don't settle. As with all
matters of the heart, you'll know when you find it . . . Have the
courage to follow your heart and intuition. They somehow already
know what you truly want to become. Everything else is secondary.

OPRAH WINFREY

What I know for sure is that if you want to have success, you can't make
success your goal. The key is not to worry about being successful, but
to instead work toward being significant—and the success will naturally
follow . . . If you do work that you love, and work that fulfills you, the
rest will come. And, I truly believe, that the reason I've been able to be
so financially successful is because my focus has never, ever for one
minute been money. Would you do your job and not be paid for it? I

would do this job, and take on a second job just to make ends meet if nobody paid me. That's how you know you are doing the right thing.

TONY ROBBINS

A real decision is measured by the fact that you've taken a new action. If there's no action, you haven't truly decided . . . The most important thing you can do to achieve your goals is to make sure that as soon as you set them, you immediately begin to create momentum. The most important rules that I ever adopted to help me in achieving my goals were those I learned from a very successful man who taught me to first write down the goal, and then to never leave the site of setting a goal without first taking some form of positive action toward its attainment . . . For changes to be of any true value, they've got to be lasting and consistent. Any time you sincerely want to make a change, the first thing you must do is to raise your standards . . . If you don't set a baseline standard for what you'll accept in life, you'll find it's easy to slip into behaviors and attitudes or a quality of life that's far below what you deserve . . . Whatever happens, take responsibility . . . The only thing that's keeping you from getting what you want is the story you keep telling yourself.

Refer to these (and your own favorites) as often as necessary. You're going to need them as you launch your campaign!

CHAPTER 4 HIGHLIGHTS

IMPORTANT TAKEAWAYS

- One individual can begin a movement that turns the tide of history.

- When you give people an opportunity to be a part of something important, they jump on board.
- Start with a simple test and prove to yourself that your One Word has power. You don't have to spend months planning—just find something easy and start!
- Make it clear. Make it powerful. Make it mean something to people.
- Don't spend so much time testing the wrong things and making continuous but minor improvements that you miss testing the biggest thing of all: the core.
- I had 50 percent better results in one month with a #Believe video than I did with my old video, which took an entire year to break the hundred-thousand-view barrier.
- When you stand for something powerful, something that means something to you, something that other people can easily understand, people will share it and rally behind you.
- You owe it to yourself to try so you don't have any regrets later in life. You rarely regret the things that you try and fail at, and the upside is that you get to live your dreams.
- If you're not motivated, you won't create great work. Ask yourself: What do you hate about being an employee? Why did you start? and What do you want to be remembered for?
- Great quotes can inspire you to keep going and save you in your darkest times.
- The only way to do great work is to love what you do. If you haven't found it yet, keep looking. Don't settle.

COMING UP: *In chapter 5, I'll run through the planning checklist to help you organize your campaign and apply your One Word to your business.*

THE PLANNING CHECKLIST

Write your goals down in detail and read
your list of goals every day ... This will keep
your subconscious mind focused on what
you want step by step.

—*Jack Canfield (coauthor of the bestselling
Chicken Soup for the Soul series)*

GETTING STARTED

There are only two mistakes one can make along the road to truth;
not going all the way, and not starting.

—*Buddha (a sage on whose teachings Buddhism was founded)*

Here is everything you need to get started with your campaign:

1. The right mindset
2. A powerful credo
3. Your founding story
4. Your tribe of followers
5. Rituals and gestures
6. A purposeful name
7. Knowing your enemy
8. Memorable logos, fonts, and symbols
9. An impactful sound

Read this section in order or skip to the parts that are most relevant to where you are now in your business.

You don't need *all* of these elements to be successful. Many people succeed with only a few. But the more you incorporate in your campaign, the greater your chances are of creating a powerful movement.

Let's dive in and kick off your campaign!

1. THE RIGHT MINDSET

Changing the game is a mindset.

—*Robert Rodriguez (American filmmaker and musician)*

Before going any further, we need to address your mindset.

When most people see the word "campaign" they think of a marketing campaign or an advertising campaign.

Something short and one-off.

Finish it and move on to something else.

This is way more important.

The origins of the word "campaign" can be traced to the late Latin word *campania*, meaning "level ground," and the French word *campagne*, meaning "open country."

You're not just running a quick marketing project.

You're Julius Caesar starting his campaign to take over the world.

You're Martin Luther King starting his campaign for equality.

You're Mother Teresa starting her campaign to end poverty.

It has to be that important.

You have to really care about this and make it powerful if you want to make an impact and have people follow you.

Remember, you are starting on "level ground" and there is nothing but "open country" ahead of you.

Don't let your past, your environment, your peers, your judgments, or the voices inside your head keep you in place and hold you back from doing something great.

Imagine what the better world you're trying to create looks like and believe in your heart that you can will it into existence. Feel the power running through your veins.

While you're in that mindset, you need to create your credo.

2. A POWERFUL CREDO

For the poet the credo or doctrine is not the point of arrival but is, on the contrary, the point of departure for the metaphysical journey.

—*Joseph Brodsky (poet and essayist awarded the 1987 Nobel Prize in Literature)*

For your campaign to be successful, you need a credo to energize yourself and the people you reach.

Your credo adds clarity to what your One Word means and the changes you are trying to make to the world.

Your credo is the message you want to pass on to your children and your grandchildren.

Your credo represents how important this campaign is.

It should motivate, inspire, and bring you to life every time you read it. When you have doubts, fears, insecurities, or a #LittleMan in your life, refer back to your credo to keep you moving forward.

Step 1: Break your One Word into three core meanings.
Whatever your One Word is, it means a few things to you. If your One Word is #Love, it might mean love yourself (self-esteem), love others (be nice), and love a higher purpose (faith).

So for you, having self-esteem, being nice, and having faith all equal #Love. That's the difference between "love" and #Love. Now it's something you can build a campaign, and later a company, around.

Step 2: Share your beliefs.
Next to each meaning, write down commands for people to follow. Make it clear what you want people to do to make your One Word campaign come to life. Make it powerful so that when you read it, your heart starts to beat faster.

So for self-esteem you might write: "Love yourself. Stop hating yourself for everything you aren't. Everyone makes mistakes, don't stop trying." Or it might be: "Love yourself. Believe that you are the sexiest thing that has ever walked this earth."

There is no right or wrong belief, just make sure it's powerful to you. Make these words to live by and pass on to future generations.

I did it for #Believe and you can too for your One Word.

MY #BELIEVE CREDO

Don't limit yourself. Many people limit themselves to what they think they can do. You can go as far as your mind lets you. What you believe, remember, you can achieve.

—Mary Kay Ash (founder of Mary Kay Cosmetics)

Here's the credo I wake up to every day and that keeps me energized:

Believe that what you're doing is right.

Follow your passion. Do it because you're meant to do it. Do it to do it, not just to make money.

Believe that you can achieve it.

Have the confidence to know that if you think you can achieve it, you can.

Believe that it will happen.

Have the conviction to follow through. Trust that if you see only darkness around you, there is light at the end of the tunnel.

It's on my website. It's in my marketing materials. It's who I am and what I hold as the truth.

It's the world I want to create and the message I continually encourage people to follow.

This is what makes the difference between believe and #Believe for me.

Turn your One Word into a credo and start building momentum for your campaign.

Your credo is the inspiration behind everything you create, including the next important step: creating your founding story.

3. YOUR FOUNDING STORY

I want customers to know and relate to me as an individual, and to understand that my company is a reflection of myself.

—Lillian Vernon (founder of Lillian Vernon Corporation, the first company started by a woman to be traded on the American Stock Exchange)

Your story is important—way more important than you likely give it credit for.

People buy from people. People follow people. People love people. They don't buy, follow, and love companies anywhere close to the same way.

If you want to build a great campaign, you need to tell your founding story.

Tell me why you're doing this. Tell me why it's important to you. Tell me how you're trying to make the world a better place. What does your One Word mean to you?

Let me feel your passion.

Telling your story helps people connect to you, and the instant they connect with you personally, they're much more likely to take action.

Because now they care.

This is one of the biggest mistakes many entrepreneurs make.

They hide behind their website and marketing materials. They don't want to make it all about themselves. They don't have huge egos. They want to make the products and services shine, not themselves.

Big. Mistake.

Telling your story isn't about boosting your ego.

Your story adds value and context for your customers.

By understanding why you started this business, I connect with the products you're selling. By feeling your passion for what you do, I connect with the quality of your products. By telling me what you stand for and are trying to accomplish, I connect with you as a person and an entrepreneur.

If you don't tell me, I don't connect. I'm going to base my decision on price. And being the lowest-priced provider is usually a death trap for entrepreneurs.

I know because that was almost me.

MY FOUNDING STORY

> If you can shape your business life or your working life, you can just
> look at it as another extension—you just fulfill all your values as a
> human being in the workplace. If you are an activist, you bring the
> activism of your life into your business, or if you love creative art,
> you can bring that in.
>
> —*Anita Roddick (founder of the Body Shop and pioneer of ethical
> consumerism)*

I never wanted to tell my story.

When I started my website, I wanted to build a great resource to help entrepreneurs succeed. I started with stories of famous entrepreneurs like Bill Gates, Oprah Winfrey, and Walt Disney because their stories inspired me.

When I was down, when I doubted myself, when I felt like I wasn't going to make it—I looked to their stories and they motivated me to keep going.

Bill Gates's story saved my business and made me stick with being an entrepreneur.

I wanted to share that knowledge with others so they could also be motivated to continue to pursue their dreams. I created an awesome website, but people kept writing in, saying: "Love the site, but who is Evan Carmichael?"

"I'm nobody compared to the entrepreneurs I'm profiling," I thought. But people were asking, so I started to share.

And my business took off.

Suddenly I was attracting more clients, more website traffic, more social media followers. I was selling more products, getting more newsletter sign-ups, receiving more media requests for interviews. I was having more fun too. :)

The product I had was already great, but when I told my story it added more context. It made it more valuable. It connected with people.

When I talk about how I was making three hundred dollars a month in my first business and Bill Gates's story saved my company and helped me build an international business and get acquired just a couple of years later, that adds context. People really want to hear what I have to say.

I realized that telling my story wasn't about me pumping myself up; it humanized my business and made it easier for people to take whatever next step I was asking them to take.

It's time for you to write your story.

YOUR LIFE, YOUR BIZ, YOUR BIO

Humans are kind of story-propagating creatures. If you think of how we spend our days, think of all the time you spend on entertainment. How much of your entertainment centers around stories? Most pieces of music tell stories. Even hanging out with your friends, you talk, you tell stories to each other. They're all stories. We live in stories.

—*Patrick Rothfuss (writer of epic fantasy and college lecturer)*

Most people's bios are boring. Superboring.

I don't want to read your résumé. That doesn't inspire me to feel anything.

Your story has to have passion, entertain, and connect me to you. Here are some elements to include:

- Your One Word and what it means to you
- Milestones you're proud of
- Personal and company goals

- Hobbies
- Marital/family status
- Favorites (sports, food, music, books, movies, travel spot)
- How and why you got started
- Your early struggles, fears, doubts
- How you got your big break
- Where you are now
- Where you are going

Make it interesting. Make it personal. Make me care about you.
Create two versions of your bio to connect with the widest audience possible.

Make the first one full length. Tell me the whole story and don't leave anything out.

The second one is a hundred-word bio. Condense everything into one hundred words.

This is a teaser that you can use for people to make them want to learn more. Show the short one first, to arouse curiosity, then the longer form below for people to dig into.

When the media is talking about you or when emcees are introducing you as a keynote speaker (remember, you're a game changer in the making) then the hundred-word version is perfect.

I use both versions every day in my business.

99 WORDS

Put it before them briefly so they will read it, clearly so they will appreciate it, picturesquely so they will remember it and, above all, accurately so they will be guided by its light.

—Joseph Pulitzer (newspaper publisher best known for founding the Pulitzer prizes)

Here's my ninety-nine-word bio:

> I #Believe in entrepreneurs.
> At nineteen, I built, then sold, a biotech software company.
> At twenty-two, I was a VC helping raise $500k to $15mil.
> I now run EvanCarmichael.com, a popular website for entrepreneurs.
> I breathe and bleed entrepreneurship.
> I'm obsessed.
> Aiming to help one billion entrepreneurs.
> Change the world.
> I've set two world records, use a stand-up desk, ride a Vespa, raise funds for Kiva, wear five-toe shoes, and created Entrepreneur trading cards.
> I speak globally but Toronto (#EntCity) is home.
> I love being married, my son, salsa dancing, DJing, League of Legends, and the Toronto Blue Jays.

Do you feel like you know me just a little bit better?
Exactly.

It works for me. It can work for you. And it can help you build your tribe.

4. YOUR TRIBE OF FOLLOWERS

The secret of leadership is simple: Do what you believe in. Paint a picture of the future. Go there. People will follow . . . Leaders lead when they take positions, when they connect with their tribes, and when they help the tribe connect to itself.

—*Seth Godin (author of multiple bestselling books, including* Tribes)

If you want to build a successful campaign, you need to connect a loyal fan base to yourself, your business, your cause, and each other.

The Grateful Dead had Deadheads. The Toronto Maple Leafs have Leafs Nation. Hulk Hogan had his Hulkamaniacs. Lady Gaga has her Little Monsters. Welcome to the world of tribes.

These are the superfans who love what you do and can't imagine a world without you. Having a tribe gives people an identity. It makes people feel closer to your cause. It ties people together. It gives them something to talk about. It makes them feel like your cause is their cause.

Here's how to leverage your tribe:

Name them.

Just like the Hulkamaniacs, Leafs Nation, and Little Monsters have names, so should your tribe. A name gives legitimacy. It makes it official. It makes people feel like they belong to something and that they're not alone. Give them a powerful name that they can get behind and spread for you.

Recognize them.

At the start, your fans are alone. It takes a lot of guts for them to stand up and tell people about something new. So support them. Recognize them. If they talk about you, make a video, write an article, buy your products—say thank you! Encourage them and they'll continue spreading your message. Make them feel special.

Bring them together.

Turn your fans from loners into belongers. Give them opportunities to meet and collaborate with other fans. Provide experiences to energize them and work on joint projects. By meeting and connecting with each other, fans become more devoted, empowered, and willing to promote you.

They should feel like they are part of an important team with you.

#BELIEVETEAM

> A deep sense of love and belonging is an irreducible
> need of all people.
>
> —Brené Brown (bestselling author, public speaker, and research professor
>   at the University of Houston)

I had my One Word but didn't have a name for my community.
Then came Charles Graham, a member of my YouTube audience who left this comment on one of my videos:

Awesome example! I'm feeling motivated! Ready to make big
moves! Believe Team!

#BelieveTeam was born!
Now when people engage with my business, I welcome them to our tribe, making them feel like they are a part of something special. Here's an example of an exchange with a recent YouTube commenter:

Joe Davey: *"Hi Evan, I've been watching your videos for a few months now and I want to say thank you! Thank you for all this great information, this has really helped me focus on thinking positively and to #Believe in everything I do."*

To which I replied: *"Awesome Joe—thanks for leaving a comment— great to have you on the #BelieveTeam :)"*

#BelieveNation
I also use #BelieveNation when making an address or referencing the entire tribe, and they use it too because they now self-identify with it. Here's an example from another YouTube commenter:

Radyo Music: *"I was reading your comments, seeing how honest everyone is . . . it's like a focus group lol."*

To which I replied: *"Yeah! #BelieveNation rocks :)"*

And another viewer, James Bailey, followed up with: *"BELIEVE NATION gives Evan Carmichael a big thumbs up"*

Giving your tribe names gives them power, belonging, and meaning. Start!

NAME THEM: TRIBUTES

We need to unite the people out there ... We can't do that without a lightning rod. The people will follow her. She's the face of this revolution.

—*Plutarch Heavensbee (in* The Hunger Games)

The Hunger Games is one of the most successful book and film series of all time.

It has brought in billions of dollars and has a hard-core group of fans that wanted to belong and take their involvement deeper, so a community was born.

The franchise, realizing the importance of naming their tribe, then took to Facebook to ask its community what they would like to call themselves.

They posted:

"OK Hunger Games fans ... there's been a lot of talk about what our nickname should be. Some call us Tributes, some call us Jabberjays. What would you call us?

Immediately the comment floodgate opened. People responded with answers like:

WE ARE TRIBUTES OR YOU CAN CALL US REBELS!
TRIBUTES x 3!!!!!!!!!!!!!!!!!!!!!!!! :)
The Hunger Gang
i like tributes but i cant kill anybody
Tributes all the way!

Almost a thousand comments came pouring in.

The winning name?

Tributes.

The *Hunger Games* tribe now had its identity.

Naming them helps, but you also need to recognize them.

RECOGNIZE THEM: CRISTAL

We used their brand as a signifier of luxury and they got free advertising and credibility every time we mentioned it. We were trading cachet. But they didn't see it that way.

—Jay Z (one of the most financially successful hip-hop artists
  and entrepreneurs in America)

Here's an example of what *NOT* to do.

Cristal is the brand name of a champagne known for its high price and exclusivity.

In the mid-1990s, and early 2000s, a tribe of rappers was influencing hip-hop culture to buy the product. Jay Z, 50 Cent, Biggie Smalls, Puff Daddy, Tupac Shakur, and others all referenced the brand in their songs.

This is where Cristal could have recognized, named, and brought together this new tribe.

Instead it did the exact opposite. It insulted them.

In a 2006 interview, Frédéric Rouzaud, the managing director of the company that makes Cristal, was asked what he thought about rappers promoting his drink. His response:

That's a good question, but what can we do? We can't forbid people from buying it. I'm sure Dom Pérignon or Krug would be delighted to have their business.

Jay Z's response?

It has come to my attention that the managing director of Cristal, Frédéric Rouzaud views the "hip-hop" culture as "unwelcome attention." I view his comments as racist and will no longer support any of his products through any of my various brands including the 40/40 Club nor in my personal life.

Jay Z called for a boycott of Cristal and started promoting a new champagne, Armand de Brignac, nicknamed Ace of Spades after its logo.

He lifted the brand from relative obscurity to being a new hit drink.

The champagne sold out of its initial production run and all future ones as well.

In 2014 Jay Z bought the Armand de Brignac business and continues to promote the champagne.

Cristal turned one of its biggest fans and promoters into a competitor by not recognizing and bringing the rap community together.

BRING THEM TOGETHER

Everything was an experience we will never forget. By the last day there was a spirit of camaraderie that was amazing. Even though we had not met any of the participants in the past we felt that we had made new friends with everyone by Saturday night.

—Pete McLallen (Jeep Jamboree participant)

Bringing your tribe together strengthens their bond and loyalty.

Jeep Jamboree

Jeep is a car company known for its sport-utility and off-road vehicles. Jeep encourages people to "live the Jeep life" and hosts Jeep Jamborees to bring customers together for off-road adventures over a weekend. They started in 1953, across the Sierra Nevada mountains, and have been running ever since. They're a chance for Jeep owners to connect with other enthusiasts, learn more about their Jeeps, and have fun at the same time.

League of Legends Viewing Parties

League of Legends is a video game published by Riot Games. Its players are usually isolated, logging in from their home computers, by themselves, to play. To combat the loneliness, Riot Games created Viewing Parties to bring players together to watch the best face off against one another. Riot Games used the Staples Center in Los Angeles for its 2013 World Championship Finals and sold out the entire stadium within one hour of putting the tickets on sale. Over thirty-two million people ended up watching the event online and at viewing parties around the world.

Not all community building has to take place in a physical location. You can also bring people together online to bond, share experiences, and strengthen ties to your brand.

Oprah's Book Club 2.0

Oprah Winfrey is a talk-show host, entrepreneur, and philanthropist best known for her talk show, *The Oprah Winfrey Show*. On September 16, 1996, she created Oprah's Book Club to discuss a new book once a month with her viewers. She single-handedly turned many obscure books into national bestsellers. In 2012 the club moved online. Her hope was to create the largest book club in the world. Members are encouraged to buy the books, connect with other members, create local book clubs, and engage with their study guides.

Whether it's offline or online, bringing your community together is powerful.

Then you can give them rituals to follow to strengthen the bond.

5. RITUALS AND GESTURES

Rituals, anthropologists will tell us, are about transformation. The rituals we use for marriage, baptism or inaugurating a president are as elaborate as they are because we associate the ritual with a major life passage, the crossing of a critical threshold, or in other words, with transformation.

—*Abraham Verghese (bestselling author and professor of theory and practice of medicine at Stanford University Medical School)*

Rituals and gestures help transform your customers into superfans.

They are the glue that holds a passionate base together. Here are some popular rituals and gestures that you might recognize:

Corona and Lime Wedges

You serve your friends Corona beer with a wedge of lemon or lime in the neck of the bottle. Corona has never explained where the tradition originated, adding to the mystery.

Oreo Twist, Lick, and Dunk

Just like there's a proper way to drink a Corona, there's a specific way you're supposed to eat an Oreo cookie. You twist off the top, lick the inside, and dunk it in milk. Twist, lick, and dunk has even become a popular game for your phone, in which you can play with virtual Oreos.

Saab Greetings

Saab buyers are obsessed with their cars. When Saab owners see each other on the road, the tradition is to wave, beep, or flash their lights. In other words, recognize them and they'll recognize you back while you both celebrate the brand and your purchase.

Gatorade Showers

When a team wins the Super Bowl, what's the first thing you see the players do? Grab a huge bucket of Gatorade and dump it over the coach's head. It's not water. It's not Powerade. It's not an energy drink. It's Gatorade. It has become known as the "Gatorade shower," "Gatorade dunk," or "Gatorade bath."

Whether you create the ritual and gestures yourself or support your fans who create them for you, they're an important part of building your brand and your community.

I use rituals and gestures in my business too.

#BELIEVE RITUALS AND GESTURES

What you do speaks so loud that I cannot hear what you say.

—*Ralph Waldo Emerson (essayist, lecturer, and a linchpin in the American Romantic movement)*

When I learned about the importance of rituals and gestures, I wanted my own!

But what ritual would represent #Believe? I found the answer on my YouTube channel. One of the things I've found about entrepreneurs is that we like to set routines for ourselves. We have a list of things we'd like to do in our morning routine. For example, we might want to wake up, go for a run, have a healthy breakfast, meditate, clean up, and head to the office. I've found in particular that when you do the first part of the routine (in this case running), you're more likely to follow through on the rest of the routine. You feel good for checking off that first box, and you're way more likely continue checking off the rest. Likewise, if you don't do the first part of the routine, you're likely to fall off and skip the rest of the list. If you don't do that run, then you eat a crappy breakfast, skip your meditation, and figure you can clean up tomorrow. You write off the entire day. Does that sound familiar?

I wanted to be a lightning rod to help keep people on routine.

The first item on the list therefore has immense importance. I wanted to give people something so simple to do that when they did it, they would feel a quick hit of accomplishment, check off that box, and continue on with the rest of their routine as planned. I also wanted to build public accountability and encouragement.

#BTA was born.

Members of #BelieveNation are encouraged to start their day with my YouTube channel, watch a video, and leave a comment. Each time they do this, they end their comment with #BTA (stands for "Believer Taking Action") and a number. The number goes up with each consecutive day they comment. So the first day is #BTA1, second day is #BTA2, and so on. If they skip a day, they start back at #BTA1. It's an easy way to start your day, helps you get on track, the videos give you a hit of motivation, and the rest of the #BelieveTeam is cheering you on as your numbers rise making you want to keep doing it. It's amazing to see the difference it's making in people's lives, mostly because they continue doing the rest of their daily routine.

And what about #Believe gestures?

Check out my YouTube channel to see what I do when I say #Believe at the end of a video or my gesture with a "shot" of #Entspresso. :)

#Believe rituals and gestures help my community feel connected, but does my name play a part in the success?

6. A PURPOSEFUL NAME

What's in a name? That which we call a rose
By any other name would smell as sweet.

—*William Shakespeare (widely regarded as the greatest writer in the English language)*

Chances are you were given the wrong advice about naming your business.

Many people will tell you to pick a name that tells what you do. Something that describes your business so people know instantly what you're all about.

That's classic Feature Selling, as opposed to Core Selling, as described in part 1.

Here's a better way: don't say what you do in your name.

Instead of picking a straightforward descriptive name, it's more powerful to *assign meaning* to a name, and there are two ways to do this.

1. **Put your One Word in your name.**

    The first method is to name your business after your One Word when the meaning is obvious. For example, naming your business the Honest Company takes the rich meaning of #Honest and attaches it to your company. People know what you stand for and have expectations for what kind of business you will be.

    But you don't *need* to name your business after your One Word. That would lead to a pretty unoriginal world—and we love being creative as entrepreneurs.

2. **Use a name without intrinsic meaning and apply meaning to it.**

    The other method is to use a name that doesn't have rich meaning and assign meaning to it. For example, tech giant Hewlett-Packard was named after its founders, Bill Hewlett and Dave Packard. The name is ambiguous and doesn't have any intrinsic meaning other than its relation to two people. Do they sell lawn equipment? Are they a dog kennel? Do they manufacture pianos? They didn't call themselves Computers 4 U, which would have been much clearer. What Hewlett-Packard did was assign meaning to its name. It created "the HP way," which was its core ideology for how staff and customers should be treated, as well as the company's responsibility to give back to the community. Employees wanted to work for it, customers wanted to buy from it, suppliers wanted to work with it—all because it stood for something important.

The name means more than just what the company sells. It is flexible. Yours should be too.

GREAT NAMES ARE FLEXIBLE

Stay committed to your decisions, but stay flexible in your approach.

—*Tony Robbins (life coach, self-help author, and motivational speaker)*

The business plan that you have right now will likely not be the business plan that makes you successful.

Most successful businesses change their products, services, and business models multiple times from the start of the business to the point where they are successful and making a big difference in the world.

Wrigley started off selling soap and baking power before getting into the chewing gum business.

BMW began as an aircraft manufacturer (that's why its logo is an airplane propeller with the blue part representing the sky) before moving to motorcycles and then cars.

Milton Hershey launched a caramel business and failed at it five times before getting into chocolates.

Ferruccio Lamborghini started in tractors and moved into cars after Enzo Ferrari told him he was just a tractor maker and knew nothing about sports cars.

On and on and on . . .

Having a name that doesn't say what you do allows you to change what you sell, even though your One Word core value remains the same.

Imagine if Hewlett-Packard called itself Palo Alto Oscillators (its first financially successful product was an audio oscillator)?

What if it wanted to expand beyond Palo Alto?

What if it decided to make new products besides just oscillators?

A name like that is limiting in every respect. It limits how your customers see you and, more important, it limits how you see yourself.

Instead, a name like Hewlett-Packard allowed the company to be free—to apply "the HP way" to anything it wanted to get into and to build a multibillion-dollar company.

I almost made that mistake with my business.

EVANCARMICHAEL.COM

My name is Adam Sandler. I'm not particularly talented. I'm not particularly good-looking. And yet I'm a multimillionaire.

—*Adam Sandler (Hollywood actor whose films have collectively grossed over $2 billion at the box office)*

I used to hate that I named my business after my name.

It was actually one of my biggest regrets early on in my career.

I started EvanCarmichael.com after I had sold my software company. I was a young entrepreneur whose business had just been acquired, and I got a fair bit of media exposure as well as requests to speak at events. So I used the website to talk about where I was going to be speaking and some of the lessons that helped me.

I never expected it to become a new business.

I wish I could say that I had this big master plan and knew how it was all going to work out, but the reality is that I had no idea. I knew I wanted to help entrepreneurs. But I wasn't attached to any "how." I started posting articles with my thoughts to my website. Then other people wanted to join. Pretty soon I had hundreds of people contributing to my site, and I realized I could make money from this by selling advertising.

It was at that point that I kicked myself.

Why did I name this thing EvanCarmichael.com? How will I ever sell it if it's got my name? Why didn't I pick a name that described what I did and would be more search-engine and keyword friendly, like Small Business Strategies? Should I rebrand now? I've already put so much work into my website and have so much momentum that it would be a shame to change it. I wish I had been smarter.

Man, am I ever glad I kept it under my name.

As my business has grown, I've found that it's a constant reflection of who I am. As my interests change, so does my business. I'm also not restricted to providing small business strategies. Having the business under my name has allowed me to build a personal brand and have people connect to me as an individual in a way that would be much more difficult under a boring, corporate identity.

I named my business after myself, without a real plan. Then I thought it was one of my biggest mistakes. Now I realize it was one of my greatest wins.

I got lucky—and also didn't have a book like this. Hopefully you can be a little more strategic. Lots of big brands have similar stories as well.

HOW BRANDS GOT THEIR NAMES

It wasn't even called Amazon.com, it was called Cadabra, Inc.—as in abracadabra . . . I had phoned a lawyer on the way to Seattle from a cell phone to incorporate the company. He said, "What do you want the company to be called?" and I said "Cadabra." And he said, "Cadaver?" and I knew that was a bad name. We changed it a few months later.

—*Jeff Bezos (billionaire cofounder of Amazon.com)*

Here's how some of the most valuable brands in the world got their names.

Apple—The initial name suggestion was Matrix Electronics. Founder Steve Jobs loved to eat apples and also used to work at Atari and wanted to be ahead of them in the phone book. He had to file a name with the government and told his team they would go with Apple unless someone else came up with a better name by 5:00 p.m. that day. They stuck with Apple.

Virgin—Richard Branson was going to call his new business Slipped Disc until one of his team members suggested that since they were all young and virgins in business, why not call it Virgin?

Google—Founders Larry Page and Sergey Brin originally called their company BackRub because it looked at backlinks to estimate the importance of a website. They changed it to Google, which is a misspelling of googol, which is the number one followed by one hundred zeros, to show that search engines provided vast quantities of information.

Nike—Originally was called Blue Ribbon Sports before changing its name to Nike, after the Greek goddess of victory.

IKEA—Comes from the founder Ingvar Kamprad's initials and the first letters of the Swedish farm where he was raised, Elmtaryd, and his village, Agunnaryd.

Sony—It started as Tokyo Tsushin Kogyo and became Sony by combining the Latin word for sound, *sonus*, with "sonny," a common way to address a boy in America in the 1950s.

Founder names—Other companies, like McDonald's (Dick and Mac McDonald), Ford (Henry Ford), Disney (Walt Disney), Gillette (King Gillette), and Ben & Jerry's (Ben Cohen and Jerry Greenfield), took their names from their founders.

So whether you are naming your business after your favorite snack, a hidden meaning, a mythological character, a Latin word, or yourself, there is no single best way to do it.

Just make sure you don't say what you do.

7. KNOWING YOUR ENEMY

You have enemies? Good. That means you've stood up for something, sometime in your life.

—*Winston Churchill (widely regarded as one of the greatest wartime leaders of the twentieth century)*

Having an enemy is a catalyst for action.

Enemies inspire creativity. Enemies challenge you to work harder. Enemies motivate you to keep going.

They aren't idols you look up to and want to beat. They are the ones who stand against everything you believe in.

Batman had the Joker. Leno had Letterman. Mozart had Salieri. Martin Luther King had racism. Tupac had Biggie. Frazier had Ali. Galileo had theology. The Hatfields had the McCoys. Apple had Microsoft. The Yankees have the Red Sox. Dogs have the postman.

Whether your enemy is a person, company, concept, idea, philosophy, or way of living, you need to find yours to give power to your campaign. Here's how:

Step 1: What's the opposite of your One Word?

If you stand *for* your One Word, then you stand *against* its opposite. If you believe in love, you are against its opposite, hate. What is the core belief, the Anti-Word, you stand against?

You can refer back to the opposites exercise (in part 1) for finding your One Word to help kick-start your Anti-Word thinking.

Step 2: Who is the face of your Anti-Word?

Now that you've found your Anti-Word, put a face to it. If America stands for freedom, its Anti-Word is oppression.

Before the American Revolution, the face would have been the British, who refused to grant independence. Any modern-day threat to freedom would be America's instant enemy.

If you stand for innovation and are trying to introduce a new product the world has never seen before, your enemy could be the big, traditional companies that are doing things the same old way.

Enemies give you power.

Find your enemy and create a rallying cry for positive change, just like I did.

MY BIGGEST ENEMY EVER

A wise woman refuses to be anyone's victim.

—Maya Angelou (bestselling author and poet)

I knew I needed an enemy for my campaign but couldn't think of one.

I'm not the kind of guy to go around making enemies.

My One Word is #Believe. The work I do is to believe in others. This doesn't lend itself to creating enemies.

So I named my enemies the Non-Believers. I quickly made a YouTube video called "Ignore the Non-Believers." The concept was right but the name was weak.

I needed something stronger. More impactful. More meaningful.

Then I remembered Harry.

But first . . . a story:

I wanted to create a motivational video for entrepreneurs because I know how hard it is to wake up every day and follow your dream, especially when the people around you may not support you.

I spent five months trying to make my goal work. I had the goal but didn't have the skills or the know-how.

I needed help.

I reached out to people I knew, asked friends for help, looked at who the best people in the world at doing these videos were.

I made it my goal. I made it important. And slowly things started to happen.

After a lot of questioning looks and rejections, I found my team and got to work.

We made a great video.

I watched it and felt like "Man, I'm honored that my name is on this." It felt sooooo good. It was six minutes and three seconds of pure awesome. So I showed it to some people in the video and publicity business, including Harry.

Harry's response?

HARRY THE DREAM KILLER

Please tell me you actually understand how the Internet works.

—*Harry (the #LittleMan inspiration)*

I was so proud of what I had just made and Harry wanted to crush it.

His response was seven words: *"No video should be six minutes ever."*

So I wrote back, showing that all the TED talks, which are extremely popular, are over six minutes.

His response?

"The average length of the top fifty videos on YouTube was two minutes, fifty-four seconds. Please tell me you actually understand how the Internet works."

So, by his logic, because the average popular video is 2:54, my video can't be 6 minutes and be popular? It's comical.

But it's also really important.

You see, the younger Evan might have listened to him. After all, this guy was an "expert" in making videos and in getting publicity. You should always listen to expert advice, right? I'd never made a video like this before, so what did I know?

Here's what I knew.

When I set my goal, I was excited about it. I felt like it was something that people needed—that I needed. The finished product was something I was so proud of creating. I wasn't about to let Harry take my goal away from me. Even if he was an expert. Even if he knew what he was talking about.

When you find something that you're passionate about, you have to keep going. Even when people tell you you're crazy. Even when people tell you that it will never work. Even when you start to doubt yourself.

Because the world belongs to the unreasonable men and women who follow their hearts and build amazing things.

You will never be truly happy, have a real impact on this world, or make lots of money if you base your decisions on other people's thinking.

Especially when that other person is someone like Harry.

#LITTLEMAN

> The haters gonna hate, hate, hate, hate, hate. Baby, I'm just gonna shake, shake, shake, shake, shake. I shake it off, I shake it off.
> —*Taylor Swift (one of the bestselling musical artists of all time and the youngest woman ever to be included in* Forbes's 100 Most Powerful Women *list)*

Harry had me fuming!

I was angry at myself that a person like Harry was in my life. More important, I was upset that people like Harry existed. Because he's anti #Believe. He's a small-thinking dream killer, and the world doesn't need more Harrys.

So when I thought about the enemy for my campaign, I knew Harry would be a perfect fit. Not so much Harry the individual, but everything that Harry represented. I didn't want to use his name in the campaign (Harry isn't his real name either) but I wanted to use something that would represent him.

Then I remembered him and his friend calling each other "little man." I'm not sure if it was in reference to height or if it was an inside joke. It didn't matter.

#LittleMan was born.

The #LittleMan is the person who tells you why your idea won't work. He points out all the flaws in your plan and casts doubt over everything you do. He's the guy throwing popcorn at you from the stands and making jokes while you're fighting in the arena as an entrepreneurial gladiator trying to change the world.

#LittleMan took off and made the #Believe movement even more powerful. People can immediately recognize a #LittleMan in their life, and naming the enemy is way more powerful than the original Non-Believers moniker I started with.

#LittleMan has become a hashtag, a T-shirt line, a video series, and so much more. I took a very negative situation and turned it into a positive. #LittleMan will be Harry's greatest contribution to the world.

Now you need to find your enemy.

Make it personal. Make it mean something. Make him easy to rally against. Turn your anger and frustration into something powerful that gives energy to your campaigns.

Oh, and my six-minute, "way too long" video? It has over one million views and counting! :)

What was the #LittleMan so afraid of?

WHAT'S THE DOUGHBOY AFRAID OF?

It was this classic David-and-Goliath story, and it got picked up in the press, and eventually, Pillsbury backed down because they were getting so much public pressure. That's really what permitted Ben & Jerry's to be distributed across the country.

—Jerry Greenfield (cofounder of Ben & Jerry's)

Sometimes the enemy that sparks your movement is your biggest competitor.

Ben & Jerry's founders Ben Cohen and Jerry Greenfield were just a couple of hippies trying to avoid becoming simply "another cog in the economic machine." Having lived through the 1960s, they disliked big business for all of its negative social and environmental effects. With Ben & Jerry's, they were trying to fix this by doing things their way and placing a lot of importance on acting responsibly.

In 1984, big business came after the little guys.

Pillsbury, the million-dollar company behind Häagen-Dazs, began to feel threatened by the rapid growth of Ben & Jerry's. In an attempt to shut down the young upstarts, Pillsbury gave an ultimatum to the distributors of Ben & Jerry's throughout Boston: sell Häagen-Dazs or sell Ben & Jerry's, but not both.

Ben and Jerry weren't about to let this corporate giant shut them down. They had no legal options so they did what entrepreneurs do best: they got creative. They launched the now famous "What's the Doughboy afraid of?" campaign and began taking it as public as they could. From placing ads on the sides of buses to renting banner planes to fly around major sporting events, Cohen and Greenfield did whatever they could think of to gain support for their campaign. They took out a classified ad in *Rolling Stone* magazine asking readers to "help two Vermont hippies fight the giant Pillsbury corporation." Greenfield even took to being a one-man picket line outside the headquarters of Pillsbury in Minneapolis, handing out pamphlets that asked, "What's the Doughboy afraid of?" To see him in action check out evancarmichael.com /oneword/extras.

Then they came up with the idea of putting a 1-800 number on every pint of Ben & Jerry's ice cream to rally support. "We started getting like a hundred calls a night," recalls Greenfield, "most of them between the hours of midnight and 3:00 a.m." Many callers even offered to organize as groups of Doughboy busters. Public interest and media attention surrounding the issue grew, most of which portrayed Pillsbury in a negative light—here was this evil corporate giant trying to put two young hippies out of business. Eventually, all the bad press forced Pillsbury to renege on its ultimatum. That year, Ben & Jerry's sales reached over four million dollars, a 120 percent increase from the year before.

Find your enemy and use them to bring attention to your campaign and grow your business.

8. MEMORABLE LOGOS, FONTS, AND SYMBOLS

There are some teams and logos you see, no matter where you are in the world, and you know exactly who they are and what they mean.

—*LeBron James (considered one of the best basketball players of all time)*

Symbols are important components of any campaign.

Julius Caesar marched into battle with flags and had soldiers whose main role was just to carry the flags.

Jay Z and his fans form triangles with their hands to represent a diamond, a play off the word "Roc" in his company Roc-A-Fella Records.

Americans across the country, every day, pledge allegiance to the flag of the United States of America.

Your logo is a visual manifestation of your campaign.

It's the single most visible symbol that people see and remember.

It represents the good you want to create in the world and should have deep meaning.

The Toyota logo represents three hearts: the heart of the customer, the heart of the product, and the heart of the progress in technology

The Adidas logo of three stripes represents a mountain of obstacles that people need to overcome.

The Amazon logo has a smiley face to represent its mission to make customers happy and points from *a* to *z* to represent the wide array of products Amazon sells.

The IBM logo creates an equal sign in the bottom right corner to symbolize equality for the world.

Even if you're just starting out, trying to graphically communicate your One Word is an essential exercise—a challenge that will help you hone your message and refine your mission.

What symbol represents your One Word?

MY AIRPLANE LOGO STORY

When everything seems to be going against you, remember that the airplane takes off against the wind, not with it.
—Henry Ford (founder of the Ford Motor Company)

My logo has a paper airplane rising.

For me the airplane rising up represents #Believe because you're taking off on a new adventure and leaving the safety of the ground.

You're chasing your dreams and are trying to climb higher and higher.

I liked the paper airplane because at the start of any project you don't have the resources, the training, the education, the experience, the funding . . . You don't have the money to build a supersonic fighter jet to blast off with.

You've got a paper airplane.

It's flimsy, it gets knocked over, the wind bends the edges . . . But you still #Believe that you're going to make it. Because it's not about how many resources you have, it's about how resourceful you can be.

Yeah, baby!

#Believe!

I almost changed it.

When I was going through a rebranding (before I came up with my One Word), I almost changed the logo from the airplane to my signature. At the time, I felt my signature would make things more personal and would make a more intimate connection with people.

But when we put the new logo up on a test page, it just didn't feel right. It looked great but didn't get me excited. So I kept the paper airplane even though my designer didn't like it.

Looking back now, it's easy to understand and articulate. The paper airplane is #Believe. My signature isn't.

Embracing your One Word makes all the decisions you face easier—and true to you.

TRUE & CO.

The truth of things is the chief nutriment of superior intellects.

—*Leonardo da Vinci (considered one of the greatest painters and one of the most diversely talented people to have ever lived)*

Your logo can empower a generation.

True & Co. is a San Francisco–based intimate-apparel brand that wants women to feel comfortable in their own skins.

To give power to her world-changing campaign, founder Michelle Lam wanted a logo that represented her ambitions:

> *I started True & Co. in my living room with five hundred bras and the goal of empowering women to understand what flatters her specific shape best.*
>
> *We are the first company to fit women into their favorite bra with a fit quiz—no fitting rooms, no measuring tape, no photos—and to recognize that there's so much more to fit than your band and cup size.*
>
> *Joined by designer Nikki Dekker of the Lake & Stars, we set out to do everything differently.*
>
> *Together with a team of intrepid women (and men!) we are changing the way lingerie is designed, engineered, shopped for and lived in.*
>
> ***Our Logo: A Reflection of True***
>
> *In our continuing search for the ideal human proportions, we are reminded of Leonardo da Vinci and the Vitruvian man.*
>
> *Our curved letters take inspiration from the female form while the geometric foundations echo the precise mathematics behind our algorithms.*
>
> *Beauty and brains in a winning combination.*

Your logo is often the first visual introduction someone has to your business.

Make it count. Change your logo to make it powerful.

HOW ICONIC LOGOS CHANGE

> Starbucks represents something beyond a cup of coffee...
> Great companies that build an enduring brand have an emo-
> tional relationship with customers that has no barrier. And that
> emotional relationship is on the most important characteristic,
> which is trust.
>
> —*Howard Schultz (billionaire chairman of Starbucks)*

As your campaign builds, people will recognize your symbol.
The evolution of Starbucks's logo is a great example.

In 1971 there was a small picture of a siren and four words in all caps: "STARBUCKS FRESH ROASTED COFFEE."

In 1987, as the brand became more recognized, the siren pic-ture was simplified and the logo was changed to only have two words: "Starbucks" and "Coffee."

In 1992 the siren picture was further simplified.

In 2011 the brand became so well known that the simplified picture of the siren is now all that's needed.

You don't need to see the name Starbucks anywhere to know it's a Starbucks logo.

Other brands that evolved to no longer need text in their logos include Nike (swoosh), McDonald's (golden arches), Apple (apple with a bite taken out), and Target (archery target).

As your campaign grows in importance and prominence,

your logo will likely evolve as well, ultimately becoming something that people will recognize without any words.

Design your logo with purpose.

THE PURPOSE OF COLOR

Pink isn't just a color, it's an attitude!
—*Miley Cyrus (singer, actress, and songwriter)*

Colors have meaning.

Here is a list of colors to consider and what many people associate them with:

Red

- Danger, passion, love, excitement, boldness
- Examples: Virgin, YouTube, Rolling Stones

Black/Gray

- Elegance, power, formality, importance
- Examples: Nike, Apple, *New York Times*

Blue

- Dependability, intelligence, trust, loyalty, wisdom
- Example: IBM, JPMorgan Chase, Facebook

Orange

- Enthusiasm, happiness, creativity, success, encouragement
- Examples: Amazon, Nickelodeon, Firefox

Green

- Growth, harmony, freshness, fertility, nature
- Examples: Whole Foods, John Deere, Land Rover, Starbucks.

Purple
- Royalty, luxury, ambition, power, extravagance
- Examples: Hallmark, Barbie, Cadbury

Yellow
- Joy, happiness, energy, sunshine, cheer
- Examples: Ferrari, *National Geographic*, IKEA

My logo used to be white and blue. When I adopted #Believe, I changed it to black and orange. And it's no wonder! For me #Believe is about doing something powerful and important (black) and being enthusiastic and encouraging (orange).

What colors best represent your One Word? And how about your font?

WHAT DOES YOUR FONT MEAN?

Because I had dropped out and didn't have to take the normal classes, I decided to take a calligraphy class to learn how to do this. I learned about serif and sans serif typefaces, about varying the amount of space between different letter combinations, about what makes great typography great. It was beautiful, historical, artistically subtle in a way that science can't capture, and I found it fascinating. None of this had even a hope of any practical application in my life. But ten years later, when we were designing the first Macintosh computer, it all came back to me. And we designed it all into the Mac. It was the first computer with beautiful typography. If I had never dropped in on that single course in college, the Mac would have never had multiple typefaces or proportionally spaced fonts. And since Windows just copied the Mac, it's likely that no personal computer would have them. If I had never dropped out, I would have never dropped in on this calligraphy class, and personal computers might not have the wonderful typography that they do.

—*Steve Jobs (billionaire entrepreneur and cofounder*
of Apple Computer)

Fonts make you feel.

A font may make you upset or happy, sad or uplifted. The same words in different fonts make you feel differently.

Here's an example—Stencil Std versus Janda Silly Monkey.

Stencil Std
GET IT DONE

Janda SM
Get it done

The first font is serious, angry, authoritative. You think of military boot camp, personal trainers, and drill sergeants. The second font is fun, playful, cute. You think of children, princesses, and fairies.

The first is yelling at you. The second is encouraging you.

What feeling do you want to evoke from your One Word?

Make sure you use a font that supports it.

To help you pick a font, check out http://wordmark.it.

You can enter a sample word and it shows you lots of variations to choose from and compare against.

If you really want to step up, you can create your own font that people instantly recognize as yours.

CREATE AN ICONIC FONT

I like thinking big. I always have. If you're going to be thinking anyway, you might as well think big... Most people think small because most people are afraid of success, afraid of making decisions, afraid of winning. And that gives people like me a great advantage.

—*Donald Trump (billionaire business magnate, investor, television personality and author)*

If you really want to go big, then create your own font.

Something that is iconic.

Something people will remember.

Something that when people see it they think immediately of you.

What do you think of when you put on a Disney movie and the name "Disney" is scrawled across the castle?

The iconic swoop in the "D" and the big dot over the "i" are instantly recognizable.

Anything written in the Disney font is immediately associated with the Walt Disney Company.

Walt Disney created a legendary business, as well as a font to go with it.

Can you be the next Walt Disney and create a unique font for your logo that will be recognized around the world?

It's possible.

You can do it.

And it doesn't have to cost a lot of money.

DON'T SPEND BIG $$$ ON A LOGO

> Don't think about the money you don't have. Rather, what can you do with what you do have?
>
> —*Steve Wozniak (inventor, electronics engineer, and computer programmer who cofounded Apple Computer)*

A logo doesn't have to cost a lot of money.

You might look at big companies like Pepsi, BBC, and BP spending millions of dollars to get their logos designed, but you don't need to have deep pockets to create a meaningful logo.

Here are a few examples:

Google:
Cost nothing. Google founder Sergey Brin designed it himself. It has been through a few changes over the years, but the original concept remains the same.

Coca-Cola:
Ditto. The original logo was designed by the company's bookkeeper, Frank Mason Robinson, in 1885. It's now one of the most recognized logos in the world.

Nike:
Thirty-five dollars. Created by Portland State University student Carolyn Davidson in 1971. Nike founder Phil Knight was teaching accounting and noticed Davidson's work on an assignment so he hired her.

Twitter:
Fifteen dollars. Twitter's original logo was purchased from iStockPhoto, a crowd-sourcing design website. Its "fail whale" graphic was also purchased through iStockPhoto.

Whatever logo you go with, make sure it means something to you and makes you feel alive.

DOES YOUR LOGO FEEL?

We should make decisions in life with our hearts, not our brains, not only in music but in daily life.

—*André Rieu (Dutch violinist and conductor best known for creating the waltz-playing Johann Strauss Orchestra)*

Do. Not. Overanalyze.

Sometimes too much information isn't good. It creates too many options. Too many things to worry about. The logo you choose is important to your campaign. The symbols you use, the colors you choose, the fonts you leverage are all important. But the most important thing to remember is that it has to make you feel.

Feel with your heart instead of thinking with your head.

I picked an airplane for my logo because it felt right.

I picked orange for the color because it felt right.

I picked a version of Futura for my logo and customized it because it felt right.

If you want to express passion in your logo, you don't have to use red. If yellow feels better, then use yellow. It worked for Ferrari.

Use the advice on the previous pages as guidelines, not restrictions.

I love my logo.

You need to love your logo.

If you love it, others will too.

And that's what's really important.

That's how you make a logo into a powerful symbol.

UNLOCK THE POWER OF SYMBOLS

Mickey Mouse is, to me, a symbol of independence.

—*Walt Disney (entrepreneur, cartoonist,*
animator, voice actor, film producer, and cofounder
of the Walt Disney Company)

Every theme in your campaign should also have a symbol.

A symbol is a visual representation of an idea.

If you want people to feel something, don't just use words; use a picture.

Every product or service you launch should have its own symbol.

The big ideas you promote and stand for should have their own symbols.

The enemy of your campaign should have its own symbol.

I use symbols everywhere.

My Zhuge line of worksheets have their own symbol.

My #EntCity campaign for Toronto has a symbol.

The #LittleMan has an symbol.

One Word has a symbol.

My Believe-O-Gram campaign has symbol.

My #Entspresso YouTube series has a symbol.

My Author Soar program for business experts has a symbol.

If you're launching a campaign, have symbols.

They are memorable, visible, powerful reminders of what you've created, and they will lift your success.

You can also model success to get examples for symbols to use in your campaigns.

To see my logo, icons, and all the ones I discussed in this chapter, check out evancarmichael.com/oneword/extras.

ICONIC EXAMPLE: OL' LONELY

> Ol' Lonely's predicament is testimony to the durability and reliability of Maytag appliances. Now if only he had something to do with his days.
>
> —*Maytag advertisement*

How do you show people that you have dependable products?

You create a symbol around it. And it doesn't have to be a logo. It can be a character.

That's exactly what Maytag did with its Maytag repairman, also known as Ol' Lonely or "the lonely repairman." Ol' Lonely was created in 1967, when actor Jesse White first played the Maytag repairman in a TV commercial.

It was a time when there wasn't much that differentiated one washing machine from another. As a result, there wasn't a strong reason to buy from one company over another, except to compare price.

To combat this, Maytag wanted to remind people that its brand stood for durability and reliability. Instead of taking out ads saying, "Remember, we're the dependable brand so buy us," Maytag decided creating a symbol would be much more powerful.

It was right.

The story behind the Maytag repairman is that because Maytag products are so reliable, they never break down, so you never need to call him to come fix your appliances. As a result, he's lonely and is looking for something to do with all his free time.

The campaign worked. Maytag gained market share, became the trusted brand for decades, was able to charge premium prices, and even got the town of Newton, Iowa, to change the name of the address of its corporate headquarters to One Dependability Square.

By the end of the twentieth century, the campaign was so successful that the character became a symbol for an entire wave of professional service providers people didn't need anymore. For example, "Most people in town now have their own cars, making the local bus driver like the Maytag repairman."

If you can combine a powerful purpose with a symbol that helps tell a story, you'll be well on your way to building a lasting, impactful, world-changing brand.

Just make sure that you continue to live your One Word.

MAYTAG NO LONGER LIVES ONE WORD

From the beginning, F. L. Maytag understood that delivering on the promise, putting his mouth where his money was, was really critical and he did that.

—*Nancy Koehn (brand historian at Harvard Business School)*

The brand that built an icon around being #Dependable lost its way.

After the Maytag family sold the Newton, Iowa, appliance business in 1962, the reputation endured for the large part of the century.

However, the quality of its products began to slowly decline. This went relatively unnoticed until 1997, when the company introduced its energy-saving front-loading washer, the Neptune, appropriately dubbed the Stinkomatic by customers.

The Neptune was literally and figuratively a stinker. It produced a bad smell in clothes that owners struggled to get rid of. In addition, the machine's electronics were poorly designed and the appliance made strange noises. Maytag was slow to respond to customer complaints and also changed its marketing strategy to encourage consumers to buy new Maytag machines before their old ones had worn out.

It was official—they were no longer living up to their #Dependable reputation.

Customer dissatisfaction grew, and then began to spread. Complaints about the Neptune and Maytag's customer service echoed throughout online forums and rating sites.

Maytag didn't anticipate the power of the Internet, and its ability to spread the company's new negative reputation. Unhappy customers united online, and eventually the negative buzz led to multiple class-action suits against Maytag that were settled with over $33 million in payouts. In less than ten years, Maytag's long-standing reputation for having the most reliable appliances was destroyed. In April 2006, Maytag was acquired by Whirlpool, and a year later the original Maytag plant in Newton was shut down.

Whirlpool held on to the Maytag brand name and reintroduced the Ol' Lonely symbol as a younger, more attractive repairman. This newer version of the Maytag Man is a tongue-in-cheek metaphorical representation of the machine itself, implying through humorous advertising that machines are more dependable than man. Time will tell whether Maytag can recapture the #Dependable position with consumers again.

It could start by pairing its symbol with an impactful sound that represents its One Word.

9. AN IMPACTFUL SOUND

I think of myself as a film composer.

—*John Williams (legendary music composer who has created some of the most recognizable film scores in history including those for* Star Wars, Jaws, *and* Indiana Jones)

John Williams made over $80 million in a single year.

Because Hollywood producers know that along with having a story, an enemy, and visuals, you need iconic music.

Entrepreneurs could learn a lot from the movies about how to create successful campaigns around their One Word.

The more senses you can engage, the more likely your company will stay in your customer's mind. This is especially true in a digital world where people can't touch and feel your products.

Music is language and it can be used to make people feel something about your business. You want to think about what sounds best convey the feeling of your One Word and how music can help people feel your message more powerfully.

You can also play with the visuals in your logo to create a complementary sound. For instance, if your One Word is #Trust and your logo is a lock, your iconic sound might be someone locking a door. If your One Word is #Love and your logo has a heart, your iconic sound might be a kiss.

In the marketing world it's called "audio branding."

It should be something short, memorable, and immediately recognizable as *your* sound to people who have heard it before. They should be able to tell the message is yours even if they close their eyes and just listen. You can even go so far as to register it as a sound trademark.

When you've found your iconic sound, you want to incorporate it wherever you have sound options in your campaigns. For example, YouTube channels, events, websites, voice mails, in-store promotions, TV or radio or online commercials, conferences, social media, and instructional videos.

Anywhere you can use sound, you want to strategically place your iconic sound to reinforce your message and get people to feel closer to your brand.

I struggled in creating my iconic sound but eventually

found something I was so proud of that I started using it on a daily basis.

WHAT DOES #BELIEVE SOUND LIKE?

Never give up trying to build the world you can see, even if others can't see it. Listen to your drum and your drum only. It's the one that makes the sweetest sound.

—*Simon Sinek (author best known for popularizing the concept of "the golden circle" and to "start with why")*

It started with my YouTube videos.

I was making regular videos for my YouTube channel and wanted an intro to kick-start each one. I didn't really have a plan or reason. Everyone else had intros, so I felt like I needed one as well. I only later understood how important it is.

So I asked my video producer to put something together. He took our logo, made it look 3-D, and had it rotate while a few bars of music played. It wasn't iconic. It wasn't developed with a strong purpose. But we had an intro. Woo!

I stuck with that sound for over a year. I liked it but I didn't love it. It was the classic story of good being the enemy of great. If it was really bad, I'd have changed it immediately, but because it was good, I just left it and didn't pursue great. I felt there were other priorities to focus on in my business.

Then came #Believe.

Once I had discovered my One Word, #Believe, everything started to change in my business and I knew I had to change my sound as well. I wanted something iconic. I wanted something people would remember.

I wanted something #Believe.

The first step was playing off the airplane. I've already discussed where my airplane logo came from, and I felt that my iconic sound should have something to do with the logo.

I gave super-unclear instructions to my video editor, Christina, and asked her to make me a new intro. My instructions were unclear because I was unclear. All I knew was that I wanted a plane.

So she came back with the plane from my logo flying across the screen with an airplane sound and then the logo showed up on screen.

The only problem was that it sounded like a crop duster was flying across the screen. This wasn't going to work.

I wanted something more powerful.

THE POWERFUL SOUND OF ONE WORD

A camel makes an elephant feel like a jet plane.

—*Jackie Kennedy (first lady of the United States from 1961 to 1963)*

I told Christina that the sound we used for our intro had to be more empowering, more inspirational, more #Believe.

That's where your One Word comes in handy. Every decision you make in your business should be seen through the lens of your One Word. It gives you certainty and clarity. It's at the foundation of everything that you do.

Because Christina understood #Believe, she got to work and her next version was much closer. Now it sounded like a jet was crossing the screen.

That's what I'm talking about!

It was powerful. It was uplifting. It made you feel like taking off. But I felt it could be made even stronger and more meaningful.

That's when it hit me. We needed a sonic boom.

When a jet is picking up speed and goes faster than the speed of sound, it creates a shockwave that results in an explosive noise, otherwise known as a sonic boom.

That's what I wanted.

I wanted the paper airplane from my logo to pick up speed, fly across the screen like a jet, and then go so fast that it breaks the sound barrier and creates a sonic boom.

That was #Believe.

That's my iconic sound. It lasts for just under three seconds, and you can hear it in any of the videos I create.

It's a sound that my audience of entrepreneurs can relate to because they are paper airplanes now, but they want to turn into high-speed jets that set records and break barriers.

It was a powerful way to reinforce my message and a method that has been used by companies for decades.

I wish I had learned from them sooner. I should have studied Intel.

THE INTEL INSIDE STORY

The mnemonic (Intel Inside sound) is worth millions of dollars.

—*Walter Werzowa (Austrian composer famous for creating the Intel "bong")*

It's over twenty years old, three seconds long, and is played once every five minutes somewhere in the world.

It's one of the most recognizable sounds in the world, and Intel spends hundreds of millions of dollars promoting it each year. The iconic Intel Inside sound helped save Intel and create a globally known brand.

It started in 1989 when Intel marketed chips based on how fast they were. Typically the company had sold only through computer manufacturers, but now it wanted to reach out directly to the end customer.

Intel marketed the 386 chip as being better than the 286 chip and had consumers asking for the product by name. It forced the manufacturers to buy more Intel chips.

Then a court ruling declared that Intel did not own the trademarks for 386 or the new 486. Intel needed a new way to promote itself. It decided to move to television advertising and to create a new Intel Inside logo to support the campaign.

But the company felt like a logo wasn't enough—it needed an iconic sound to go along with the logo, so people would remember them.

In 1994 former electronica musician Walter Werzowa was tapped to create the sound. The direction he was given was that "the sound needed to convey reliability, innovation, and trust."

He spent the weekend in his LA home studio trying to come up with something but got more and more frustrated. His breakthrough came when he tried signing the words "Intel Inside" to himself and the result was the five-note iconic sound that would last for decades, known as the Intel "bong."

The bong has been rearranged a few times over the years to keep it current, but Intel has stuck with the same five notes for over two decades and has had tremendous success with it.

It has become what some consider the most played piece of music in history.

CHAPTER 5 HIGHLIGHTS

IMPORTANT TAKEAWAYS

- You don't need *all* of these elements to be successful. Many people succeed with only a few. But the more you incorporate into your campaign, the greater your chances are of creating a powerful movement.
- For your campaign to be successful you need a credo to energize yourself and the people you reach. Your credo is the inspiration behind everything you create.
- Your founding story is important. Way more important than you likely give it credit for. Your story adds value and context to your customers. Most people's bios are boring. Superboring. Make yours interesting. Make it personal. Make me care about you. It works for me. It can work for you.
- If you want to build a successful campaign, you need to connect a loyal fan base to yourself, your business, your cause, and each other. Name them. Recognize them. Bring them together. Give them rituals.
- Chances are you were given the wrong advice about how to choose a name for your business. Your name should mean more than just what you sell. It should be flexible.
- Having an enemy is a catalyst for action. Find your enemy and create a rallying cry for positive change.
- Symbols are important components of any campaign. What symbol represents your One Word? Colors have meaning. Fonts make you feel. And a logo doesn't have to cost you a lot of money.
- Every theme in your campaign should have a symbol. If you can combine a powerful purpose with a symbol that helps

tell a story, you'll be well on your way to building a lasting, impactful, world-changing brand.

- Music is language and can be used to make people feel something about your business. In the marketing world it's called "audio branding." The Intel Inside jingle has become the most played piece of music in history.

COMING UP: In chapter 6, I'll introduce you to five companies that are using their One Word to create businesses with revenues of $50,000 to $150 million a year.

PART 3

COMPANY

I really try and live the mission of the company and ... keep everything else in my life extremely simple.
—*Mark Zuckerberg*

IN PART 3: COMPANY, I'll show you *how to use your One Word* and apply it to different components of building a business, including *raising capital, marketing and branding, customer service, recruiting a team and building a culture*, and *operations*. I'll include real-world examples from successful entrepreneurs who are using their One Word to build meaningful businesses and show you how you can model their success.

ONE WORD COMPANIES

> We asked ourselves what we wanted this company to stand for. We didn't want to just sell shoes. I wasn't even into shoes—but I was passionate about customer service.
>
> —*Tony Hsieh (CEO of Zappos)*

Buckle up. The ride is about to get more exciting.

We've talked about how to find your One Word and what it means to you. We've gone into detail about how you can use your One Word to create successful campaigns to drive business growth.

That's the easy stuff. That's the low-hanging fruit, to give you a taste of what's possible. Now it's time for something much more powerful:

Build a company that matters.

Your One Word isn't just a personal philosophy. It's not just a marketing campaign. You can build world-impacting companies using it, and it can work for you no matter what size business you have.

This section will show you how five different entrepreneurs and I, with companies ranging from $50,000 to $150 million in revenue, have used our One Word to go from creating a full-time income to building game-changing empires.

Each entrepreneur is represented by a number of dollar signs, from $ to $$$$$, depending on their revenues. Feel free to read the entire section or skip to the stories most relevant to you.

The entrepreneurs are:

- Roberto Blake, a graphic designer who built a $50,000 full-time business around #Awesome ($)
- Sharon Galor, founder of Toronto Dance Salsa, a dance instruction school with $500,000 in revenue created around #Family ($$)

- Mark Drager, founder of Phanta Media, a video-production company with over $1 million in sales and whose One Word is #Extraordinary ($$$)
- Rich Sheridan, cofounder of Menlo Innovations, a software-design firm with $5 million in revenue built around #Joy ($$$$)
- Christopher Gavigan, cofounder of the Honest Company, a consumer-goods business that sold over $150 million based on #Honest ($$$$$)

It worked for them. It can work for you, no matter what size your business is.

Here we go.

CHAPTER 6

CULTURE

Businesses often forget about the culture,
and ultimately, they suffer for it because
you can't deliver good service from unhappy
employees.

—*Tony Hsieh (CEO of Zappos)*

The team you build will make or break your company.

If you want to do something big, you can't do it alone, but most entrepreneurs don't have the tools to build a culture that attracts and keeps top-level talent.

You hire someone, usually the wrong person, put so much time and energy into training and teaching them, and then they quit or you have to let them go because it's not a fit—and it wasn't really ever a fit.

Or you get people who are just good enough that you can't fire them but not good enough to get you to the next level.

Building a team is one of the most frustrating experiences for entrepreneurs, and many end up going back to doing everything themselves because they don't want the headache and at least they know things will be done right.

That's where your One Word comes in.

It's the secret ingredient that binds everything together.

In this chapter we're going to look at how you can apply your One Word to build a powerful culture in the following ways:

1. How to make the right hire
2. How to onboard new hires
3. A purposeful environment
4. Create rituals
5. Names and language
6. Policies
7. Firing

1. HOW TO MAKE THE RIGHT HIRE

When I'm hiring someone I look for magic and a spark. Little things that intuitively give me a gut feeling that this person will go to the ends of the earth to accomplish the task at hand.

—Tommy Mottola (Casablanca Records)

The hiring process is broken.

The way most companies hire is insane and extremely ineffective. Here's a typical example:

1. You need to hire a programmer so you post a job ad. It's boring and looks like every other job ad out there.
2. You quickly get bombarded with job applications, résumés, and cover letters. Most of them aren't customized and are just templates that the people use for all their applications. Many applicants didn't even read your job post. They saw "programmer" in the title so they applied. It took them ten seconds to send you an e-mail, but it might take you five minutes to read each résumé and cover letter, to weed out some of the poor applicants. One hundred applications times five minutes each is already five hundred minutes of wasted time. That's already a full

day wasted, and our example assumes that the applications come in together and you can review them all at once, which isn't going to happen.

3. Then you do the interviews. You ask the applicants about their goals, why they're interested, and their life stories. The problem here is that you're testing the wrong skills. Someone's ability to ace an interview has nothing to do with how they'll perform for you as a programmer. Days are wasted conducting and scheduling interviews, consuming your time as well as that of other members of your team. Multiple rounds usually occur, extending and delaying the process.

4. Finally you pick someone who has the best experience and did the best in the interviews. Now it's time for them to start working, but they start off as a disappointment. They're not contributing as much as you thought they would, they have views and values that don't match your own, and they grow increasingly unhappy. Your productivity drops, as does your team's.

5. You think it's a training issue, so you invest more into trying to make it better. But it doesn't. And you don't want to fire them because you just spent all this time going through the hiring process and you can't afford to fire them. And you don't want go through that hell all over again!

The hiring process is broken. It's time to fix it.

HIRING THE #BELIEVE WAY

The secret of my success is that we have gone to exceptional lengths to hire the best people in the world.

—*Steve Jobs (billionaire entrepreneur and cofounder of Apple Computer)*

I have a team of misfits.

A lot of the people on my team would have had a hard time fitting in and getting jobs in other places. But they have a home with me and work their butts off for me. As I write this, I have sixteen people on my team, each of whom contributes enormous value. In my ten-plus years in this business, I've only lost two employees who wanted to go to another company. One was a bad hire, and one wanted to come back to me after leaving.

Here's my hiring process. It's not perfect, but it's better than anything I've seen:

1. **Post the job ad, and make it ooze #Believe.** I want people to love it or hate it. Many read it and think, "That's so stupid. Who builds a business around #Believe?" Perfect! Please don't apply. Neither of us will be happy working together. I just saved hours upon hours of my time by not dealing with the wrong people.

2. **Make them do some work.** My ad is one huge, ugly paragraph with no formatting or breaks. I need people who are detail oriented (because I'm usually not) and making it harder to read forces them to pay attention. I also ask a question somewhere in the middle of the paragraph, like "When applying, please mention how many Twitter followers I have." Eighty percent of the people who apply don't include it. Fantastic! You might have the greatest experience and résumé ever, but you didn't read my job posting so I'm not going to bother reading your application. A small percentage will also ask, "Evan, what is your Twitter account?" Wow. If you don't have enough resourcefulness to search for Evan Carmichael on Twitter, it won't be a fit.

3. **No interviews.** I don't read cover letters. I don't look at applications. I don't do interviews. Because these don't

test the skills I'm looking for and they're too easy to fake. Instead, I offer a paid trial. I'll look at a typical assignment that the applicants would have to do if they were working with me and give it to them. I find something that I think will take two hours to do and give them five hours to do it. During the trial I get to see how well they work with me and my team. Do they just do what I asked or go above and beyond? Do they milk me for the full five hours or are they honest and only bill me for the two it actually took?

In the trial I usually find someone who stands out from everyone else, and usually it's someone I never would have picked if I had looked at them on paper.

This system works and is repeatable. Hire misfits who are perfect fits for you.

HIRING PERFECT FITS

I pick people specifically that I can actually help grow, so the value proposition is a win-win for other people like me, a bootstrapping entrepreneur.

—*Roberto Blake ($)*

#Awesome hiring—Roberto Blake ($): *The people I work with have to be doing something #Awesome and I'll ask them to fill out my questionnaire. Because I'm a solopreneur, I mainly work with freelancers, so I had to set criteria for what it means to do #Awesome work. I look for situations that are a win for everyone involved. I pick people I can help grow . . . other solopreneurs like me that I can collaborate with. It doesn't have* *to be a money exchange. I'm open to working with someone I can give resources to in exchange for their creative value.*

#Family hiring—Sharon Galor ($$): *New hires are nearly always customers first. Nearly all the new instructors hired started as students. They have a passion for dancing and love to help others. They start as students and then become volunteer Helpers first. They are loving to the students and make everyone feel comfortable and welcomed. It doesn't matter if they're the best salsa dancer. For us, the passion to help is always more important than putting on a show.*

#Extraordinary hiring—Mark Drager ($$$): *Our interview candidates get the chance to prove they're #Extraordinary. Each candidate is asked to fill out a survey, with the reason that we're looking for #Extraordinary people—and only half of them finish the survey! We also ask them to talk about their best manager, worst manager, and funny experiences at work. This is the only page that we'll look at. It shows if they are articulate, passionate, humorous, and have other qualities that fit in with our culture. Then I schedule ten-minute calls with those who will be a good fit, and from that we choose the ones who match up well. I invite them to interview offsite, at a coffee shop, for a more informal conversation. A technical test is next, if necessary.*

#Joy hiring—Richard Sheridan ($$$$): *We look at the human being, not the résumé. It's an open, noisy environment and we work in pairs so we designed an interview process that simulates the culture. In the "Extreme Interview" we don't ask typical questions or look at résumés. We invite around thirty people and put two candidates together with instructions to help the other* *person get a second interview. They work with one pencil and piece of paper with tips like "don't grab the pencil from the other person." It's surprising how many people fail this simple task!*

#Honest hiring—Christopher Gavigan ($$$$$): *There's one main thing we look at when hiring: why here? When we get submissions for open positions, there's a simple question we ask: Why do you want to work here; in what ways do you feel like the #Honest lifestyle and philosophy is representative of you? The answer to this question tells me so much about how they'll perform. It captures their inner joy and drive.*

Once you've found the perfect match, it's time to bring them on board.

2. HOW TO ONBOARD NEW HIRES

If you can hire people whose passion intersects with the job, they won't require any supervision at all. They will manage themselves better than anyone could ever manage them. Their fire comes from within, not from without. Their motivation is internal, not external.

—Stephen Covey (educator, businessman, keynote speaker, and author of The Seven Habits of Highly Effective People)

If you do a good job hiring, then you shouldn't need to do a lot of onboarding. You've already taken care of it in your hiring process.

You shouldn't need to get people acclimated to your culture and the way you do things because every step along the way in your hiring process you've helped them understand who you are and what you stand for.

In your job posting you made sure you talked about your One Word, what it means to you, and how you apply it, instead of just posting the same boring job ads most companies do.

In the trial job, they got to work either with you directly or with some of your team on a project that was relevant to the kind of work that they would do. They've asked you questions, gotten a sense of how you work, and should be in love with your company and mission.

If they're not, you hired the wrong person.

All that's left to do is introduce them to the rest of the team, get them up to speed on the projects they'll be working on, and train them on the additional skills they'll need to do their job.

Those aren't trivial things. They're important. But when you have the right person, with the right motivation, it's easy to teach them what they need to know, and they will be hungry to learn.

There is one last vital step to onboarding: make time for it.

If you're consistently hiring the wrong people, it may be the hiring process you're using, and fixing it can help . . . but it may also be you. Do you make personal time for new hires? This is especially important in smaller companies. Yes, you hired them to *save* you time, but that only happens once they're fully set up. As a leader, your door should always be open to helping your people succeed, especially in the first three months. They'll have more questions and need extra help. Plan for it. Don't pack your schedule as much. It'll all be worth it when they start shining brightly like the stars they are.

Here's how I onboard the #Believe way.

I #BELIEVE IN PERSONAL ONBOARDING

> Ramping up the Autopilot software team at Tesla . . . I will
> be interviewing people personally and Autopilot reports
> directly to me.
>
> —Elon Musk (billionaire CEO of Tesla Motors and SpaceX)

I hire and onboard everyone myself.

I have sixteen people on my team and my time is starting to get stretched, but I personally hire and onboard every new person who joins my business. There is a lot of collaboration between my team members, but I still personally manage everyone. Everyone reports direct to me. This will have to change as my business grows, but because bringing new people on board is among the most important things that is done in any business, that's where I still spend my time. It's high leverage.

Everything just works.

New hires typically just work with me on the test project, and I make the call on who to offer the job to. Once they're hired, I introduce them to the other people on my team they will be working with—and it just works. Everyone is on the same page. The new person is accepted as a part of the team and fits into the #Believe family quickly. People are welcoming, friendly, open, and it almost feels like the new person has been there for years. Maybe I'm just lucky, but I've never had a hire, even the bad hire, who didn't get along with everyone and fit it. I could probably do a better job of involving my existing team in the hiring of new people and also develop their hiring skills, but so far everything just works.

Give responsibility.

I hate being a micromanager. I'm not good at it, and if someone needs me to be looking over their shoulder to get work done, it's not going to be a great fit with my style of management. I'll show new people how we've always done things but express that I'm really open to their views on how things could be better. I encourage them to put their art into it. That's probably why I hired them in the first place—because they wowed me and went above and beyond in the paid trial.

I have an open door.

The first e-mails I check every day are those from my team. A lot of times they figure things out on their own without me, and I encourage them to try things on their own, but they'll still need my input on some issues. I try to thank them for their ideas, even if they're not relevant or helpful at the time, because I appreciate the effort. I also try to encourage them and build them up after a mistake. If your team feels like you've got their back, they'll work even harder to make the business shine.

Now let's look at how other companies onboard around their One Word.

ONBOARDING STEPS TO SUCCESS

In my experience as a hiring manager (at other companies), the day they interview you is the best day. It's shiny and new and I'm a perfect fit, and when you show up for the first day, they barely remember who you are, and the project got canceled, and you got stuck in the lunchroom.

—*Richard Sheridan ($$$$)*

#Awesome onboarding—Roberto Blake ($): *Clarity is the key to onboarding. First, I set clear expectations. They must be willing to give value to others, set standards, and continually grow. I will outline a process for them on how we'll work together if they don't present a plan of their own.*

#Family onboarding—Sharon Galor ($$): *Onboarding begins even before the hiring stage at Toronto Dance Salsa. Students move into volunteer positions as Helpers. Some then become Assistants before they start training to become an Instructor. By the time they're Instructors, they've been here two years and know what the culture and responsibilities are. They already know what #Family is all about.*

#Extraordinary onboarding—Mark Drager ($$$): *New hires get put to work right away. I, or a member of my team, spend the first few hours of a new hire's morning with them. I'll take them on a tour around the office for introductions and questions, get their e-mail set up, and walk through how we do things. Then I'll take the new hire out for lunch. Afterward, depending on the role, they get ready to rock!*

#Joy onboarding—Richard Sheridan ($$$$): *At Menlo, the joyful culture starts from day one. The onboarding process is part of the interview process. Candidates get a one-day paid contract on their second interview. In the third interview, they get a three-week paid contract. They are paired up, just like the staff, and work on real projects. It doesn't take long to become entrenched in our culture. New hires are ready to mentor within six weeks. Not because they know everything, but because they know six people on the team they can reach out to. Demoralizing team members in the early stages won't produce #Joy. Everyone wants this to be the job of their dreams, so I want to jolt them out of their previous experiences.*

#Honest onboarding—Christopher Gavigan ($$$$$): *It's an intense first week. Each new hire gets an in-depth office tour and are escorted up to customer service. We're different in that* *the customer service department is right in the same building, which provides a very close connection. New employees sit and listen to phone calls for a half day, where they get important insight into what drives the customer. They realize our customers are fanatical about knowing the details of our products, which provides the customer the peace of mind they're searching for. A new hire is welcomed to their own space with a signed copy of my book, as well as* The Honest Company Notebook. *I include a note to welcome them to the #Honest family and an invitation to find me at my orange desk whenever they need to.*

You have your team. Now you need to create an environment they can thrive it.

3. A PURPOSEFUL ENVIRONMENT

Our environment, the world in which we live and work, is a mirror of our attitudes and expectations.

—*Earl Nightingale (radio personality, speaker, and author, nicknamed the Dean of Personal Development)*

Your environment holds you where you are.

I could write a whole book just on this topic (hmm, not a bad idea), but your physical environment, your friends, the media you consume, the books you read, your schedule and morning routine—they all hold you where you are.

There's a reason why most people will end up like their parents. There's a reason why people say you will be the result of your five closest friends. Most people have an average environment and stepping outside it becomes uncomfortable, so you go back to the safety of what you already know.

If you want to do great things, you have to surround yourself with greatness.

And that applies to your business just as much as it does to your personal life.

You need a great environment that inspires you, great friends who push you, great books that motivate you. Otherwise you'll keep being average.

What does the physical environment look like at your office? Does it inspire you and your team to push harder, do more, and follow your One Word?

Does your environment transport you to a different world that people can't wait to come back to?

What's on the walls? What's on the floor? Is music playing? Is food offered? Do people have the tools they need to excel? Do you have a library? Do you bring in guest speakers? Do you have lunch-and-learns? Do you play games together? Do you watch and share helpful videos together?

Think about what your One Word means to you and then look at your environment. If your One Word is #Calm, do you feel calm in your environment? If your One Word is #Inspire, do you feel inspired there?

There is room for improvement in every area of your environment.

Start surrounding yourself with greatness so you can achieve greatness.

I did it for #Believe.

MY ENVIRONMENT SCREAMS #BELIEVE

Your outlook upon life, your estimate of yourself, your estimate of your value are largely colored by your environment. Your whole career will be modified, shaped, molded by your surroundings, by the character of the people with whom you come in contact every day.

—*Orison Swett Marden (author and founder of* Success *magazine, in 1897)*

I want my environment to scream #Believe.

I used to have an office and envisioned a place where I could build a team and where we could all collaborate and inspire one another to do great things. I bought an office when it was just me, but I had big dreams! As I starting growing and hiring, I built just what I had envisioned—and it was great!

But then I got hit with a surprise.

I was in my midtwenties and was the youngest person at my company. In the span of a few months, a number of my people decided they wanted to travel the world. They were young and wanted to explore. They really wanted to keep working with me, but they had to do this as a life goal.

I had a choice to make.

Either let them go and hire new people or keep all these amazing people I'd found and let them work from wherever they were. I never imagined creating a remote team, but keeping great people and letting them work on what they love while exploring the world they love just seemed like a perfect case of #Believe. So I sold my office and now we all work from home—or wherever home is at the moment.

So I had to make my home office #Believe.

I wanted to be filled with #Believe every time I stepped into my office. I put a huge #Believe logo up on the wall. I have pictures of Steve Jobs, Howard Schultz, Walt Disney, and others on the walls. I have other inspiring entrepreneurs rotating on my desktop background. I created a #Believe music playlist that I put on while I'm working. I established a morning routine that supports me and encourages me to think big and follow my dreams.

Wherever I am, it has to ooze #Believe to reinforce the mission I'm on and help me stay on track.

Your environment should ooze your One Word too. Here's how.

MAKE IT OOZE YOUR ONE WORD

Space matters a lot, and it can diminish or supplement human energy.
—*Richard Sheridan ($$$$)*

#Awesome environment—Roberto Blake ($): *My intention is to create #Awesome content, so I make it easy for me to do that at any moment. My environment is prepared with props and triggers for consistent, reliable #Awesome results. My camera is always ready to film, so I can step in at any time to create video. A huge whiteboard and calendar help keep a space for my ideas and organization.*

#Family environment—Sharon Galor ($$): *Students are welcomed as soon as they walk in. A television in the lobby is set up to play video of the volunteer Helpers having a good time. There's also an event board, where we post studio happenings and community events. Students can add their own notices, like personal gatherings and selling their old dance shoes. The studios themselves are airy rooms with mirrors. They have an intimate feeling, but they're not crowded at all. I shopped around for months to find just the right floors that were designed to slip. This really helps beginners so they are able to spin easily, regardless of their experience or proper dance shoes.*

#Extraordinary environment—Mark Drager ($$$): *I asked my team what kind of environment would produce #Extraordinary work. The old office was completely open, and I would often go to Starbucks if I needed a private meeting. Once we realized that having open and closed formats would work best, we created the new space split with a main open area for collaborations as well as some separate smaller rooms so people can work quietly.*

#Joy environment—Richard Sheridan ($$$$): *There's no secret hiding place at Menlo. Our place is an open environment designed for communication. Psychologists have proven this won't work in an environment that is about 80 percent introverts, but it does! Everyone works in a ginormous space with no cubicle walls, in a basement of about eighteen thousand square feet. Tables are clustered together, organized in groups by client projects. My team is encouraged to change and move the layout of the tables however they want, and they often do. Because the tables are pushed together, they are working shoulder to shoulder. You can easily overhear other people in the same group. This means they don't gossip and are more likely to be tolerant and respectful.*

#Honest environment—Christopher Gavigan ($$$$$): *My #Honest team thinks of colleagues as a second family. This is a place of relationships and friendships. There are times when we spend more time here than with our families. Connectivity is important, and without offices or cubicles, it's inevitable and easy. My cofounder, Jessica Alba, has also influenced the space with a feminine, fun touch.*

Now that your team has a great environment, you can give them rituals to strengthen the bond to your company and each other.

4. CREATE RITUALS

> Ritual is important to us as human beings. It ties us to our traditions and our histories.
>
> —*Miller Williams (contemporary poet and translator)*

Rituals help you design a life with purpose.

You get together with your family over Christmas and Thanksgiving. You celebrate the Fourth of July with fireworks. You give presents to people on their birthdays. You take your kids out trick-or-treating on Halloween. If you're not American, you have other rituals that are specific to your culture. You set aside time for these rituals and to spend time and celebrate with your family.

Rituals are important to business too.

Awards and ceremonies for great employees encourage the team to do better. Outside work activities like company softball teams or charity events bring people closer together. Sales rewards and contests encourage more sales. Celebrating birthdays and important milestones makes people feel important. Beer Fridays foster community building.

Rituals build and reinforce the culture you are creating.

If you want to design a powerful culture around your One Word, start by thinking about what behaviors you want to recognize, encourage, and promote.

If your One Word is #Calm, then you could create Meditation Mondays to kick-start your week with a group meditation. You could give someone the chance to pick the #Calm music for the office. You could reward the customer service rep who was most #Calm with a customer each week. Share their story and make them feel proud. People will love these rituals or hate them. And that's the point.

Your rituals define your business.

They show your team who you really are and what you really

value. Your rituals should polarize people so they can't wait to be involved or they want to run the other way. That's how you build a culture that is meaningful and effective.

I've built my company's rituals around #Believe.

RITUALS WE CAN #BELIEVE IN

I think how you start the day many times determines what kind of day you're going to have.

—*Joel Osteen (bestselling author, and the senior pastor of Lakewood Church, the largest Protestant church in the United States)*

Every Thursday I closed the office an hour early to play cards with my team.

Killer Bunnies was our game of choice. It's a game of strategy where you build up an army of bunnies to attack each other and collect carrots to determine a winner. My office was generally quiet. People talked and collaborated when needed, but otherwise we were all heads down, headphones on, crushing it on our assignments. So I wanted to have something fun that we could all enjoy, on company time, to bring the team together.

What started as a fun one-off afternoon became an important company ritual.

I don't remember who suggested the idea initially, but closing shop an hour early on one Thursday immediately became a Killer Bunnies Thursday ritual that nobody wanted to miss. It became our time to have fun, relax, and enjoy each other's company.

It became so important that back when I used to still do hiring the traditional way with job interviews, the final interview would be playing Killer Bunnies with the team to see how you fit in. No questions. Just cards. After the games, we'd pick who we wanted to work with.

It was such a part of the culture that when my programmer, Adis, went back home to Holland but continued to work for me, he asked if he could call or Skype in, so he could still be a part of our games, even though it would be 11:00 p.m. his time. One day, one of my customers was in the office on Thursday afternoon and we invited him to join the game. Since then, we had a customer at almost every single game we played. They loved joining in on our ritual, and it made them feel closer to us.

I miss those days.

My team moved all over the world, and it ended up being only two of us still in the office. It didn't make sense to keep the office, so I sold it and we moved to a virtual model. Jason, the lone local on my team, still comes over once week and we play a game together (this time it's League of Legends).

I could and should do more to bring the whole team in, even though they are around the world. Writing this section has helped clarify in my mind just how important it really is.

I'm still learning too, and here are a few great examples to model.

LEARNING TO CREATE RITUALS

We've done horseback riding, sushi making, trampoline dodgeball . . . anything you can think of to bring the #Family together, we've done.

—*Sharon Galor ($$)*

#Awesome rituals—Roberto Blake ($): *I'll pick 1-2-3 solopreneurs each day and spend ten minutes reaching out with suggestions. For* *example, a photographer needs IT help. So I tweet her a solution. #Awesome! My focus is on connecting with creators. I'm actively engaged with my people. I chat with them on Facebook, I reply to comments on YouTube. I have a ritual of awesomely engaging, every day.*

#Family rituals—Sharon Galor ($$): *Birthdays are a big deal in our #Family. For many businesses, a customer's birthday would be just another day . . . but at Toronto Dance Salsa, it's an event for the whole #Family. When celebrating a student's birthday, we pull her into the center of our dance floor, and join her in a birthday dance, each taking turns dancing with her one at a time. The whole #Family joins in. We also have regular outings for our Instructors, Assistants, and Helpers. We do everything from archery tag, to fencing, to trampoline dodgeball. Game nights and movies at the studio too.*

#Extraordinary rituals—Mark Drager ($$$): *Communication breakdowns cost you money. Every week we have a Monday morning meeting. Key people must attend. We'll go through every project in production. It's a great place for us to discover where we can brainstorm ideas, communicate better with the client, or move on to the next phase.*

#Joy rituals—Richard Sheridan ($$$$): *Storytelling is a ritual as old as mankind. It's an important part of our business culture. We tell stories every day. There's an alarm clock on the dartboard, and it goes off daily at 10:00 a.m. This signals our Stand-up Meeting is ready to start. "Bong, bong, bong"— everyone hears it and stands up to form a circle. Everyone's included: clients, guests, family members . . . whoever's with us. We pass around a plastic Viking helmet and tell our work* *stories. Because we work in pairs, it's natural for each person to grab one of the horns when their turn comes. It's a goofy, fun way to report what we are working on.*

#Honest rituals—Christopher Gavigan ($$$$$): *Thirty-minute meetings. We care about people's time, and we know we don't have time to waste. So the Honest Company has a thirty-minute ritual. We limit all meetings to that. When the senior team meets, we only talk about things that keep us excited. I have rituals for myself too. Every day, I walk through the front door because I want to greet my people. I see it as a transformative moment, to remind me of what I'm doing. Every Friday I do what I call CTG Reach Outs (CTG are my initials). I basically make fifteen customer phone calls. I like to contact both loyal and disgruntled customers.*

Rituals can also be powered up if you add unique names and language to your culture.

5. NAMES AND LANGUAGE

Words are singularly the most powerful force available to humanity. We can choose to use this force constructively with words of encouragement, or destructively using words of despair. Words have energy and power with the ability to help, to heal, to hinder, to hurt, to harm, to humiliate, and to humble.

—*Yehuda Berg (founder of the Kabbalah Center)*

The most powerful cultures create their own language.
A Starbucks employee isn't called a "cashier," "crew person,"

or "team member," like other companies might call them. Starbucks calls the frontline staff "baristas" to reflect the artisanal nature of their responsibility for brewing perfect coffee. Their role is to "create uplifting experiences for the people who visit our store and make perfect beverages—one drink and one person at a time." And so Starbucks gives them a name to match. All employees at Starbucks, regardless of their position in the company, are also called "partners" to reflect the values that the business is trying to encourage: treat this business like it's yours. They're given stock options too, so they actually are partners in the company.

Starbucks also created a language for its customers.

Where else can you order a Grande, half-sweet, no-whip, soy, pumpkin-spice, affogato-style Frappuccino? Customers who learn how to speak the language feel more connected to the company. Going to Starbucks becomes a daily ritual that they can't function without.

The result? Starbucks has become not just a well-known brand but a household word. For some, their name has become synonymous with coffee itself: they say, "I'm going to go get a Starbucks." All this has been accomplished without a national advertising campaign. The company spent a total of less than $10 million on advertising in its first twenty-five years in business.

Names and language are a critical part of every successful culture.

They make people feel included, like they are a part of a special group that they can be proud of. Unique language adds extra meaning where previously it didn't exist.

What names do you have for the people, processes, and products at your business? Do they reflect the culture that you're trying to build and inspire people to be the best versions of themselves?

Don't just default to standard names because that's what everyone uses. Make your names powerful. Fill them with meaning. And your team will respond accordingly.

What does #Believe language look like?

#BELIEVABLE LANGUAGE

The Eskimos had fifty-two names for snow because it was important to them: there ought to be as many for love.

—*Margaret Atwood (bestselling novelist, essayist, and environmental activist)*

I like to tailor job titles to the result I want from each individual I hire.

When I post new jobs, I always lead with #Believe. I'll post an ad for a #Believe video editor or a #Believe community manager. The name always attracts attention—both good and bad. It helps people self-select in, if that's who they are, and helps me find the right people to join my team. It also eliminates a lot of skeptics. Perfect!

Once hired, people get an individual job title specifically for them.

GT is our "author champion." He's in charge of working with the more than eight thousand authors who contribute articles to my website. If I were to write his job description, it would be, essentially, to answer author questions, promote our programs, and grow our base of articles. But GT does so much more than that!

I asked him to join my team because what he is great at is being a champion of people. He's always positive and encouraging. He's genuinely curious about what you do, and wants to help. He takes the time to make sure you solve whatever problem you're facing, because he actually cares about you. I could have called him our author support rep or author manager, but that's so . . . boring. It doesn't inspire him or the people he works with. Author champion fits GT. It's who he is, and every day he gets to go do what he loves and be a champion for others.

I also apply names and language to the actions I want my team and customers to take.

As an example, my authors log into an admin tool so they can add articles. Most companies might call it an "admin panel" or "author back end." And that's exactly what it is—but that's not using Core Selling. You're not building people up. You're not making them feel like they are a part of something special and can be a better version of themselves. Don't promote features or benefits—promote values.

Our admin tool is called the Author Soar Command Center. It has its own logo and font, and is designed to make our authors feel like they have the power to do something big with us. "Author" is so they know it's for them. "Soar" ties into the plane logo we have for the business. "Command Center" is to make them feel in charge and like they're about to do something powerful. Now imagine logging into that every day instead of an "admin panel." Can you feel the difference?

Names assign meaning to things. Use them to make your team come alive.

LANGUAGE FOR YOUR TEAM

I don't want to work with an "account manager." I don't want to be an account that is managed.

—*Mark Drager ($$$)*

#Awesome language—Roberto Blake ($): *It's more than a word, it's a philosophy. I want to create a legacy that I'm proud of and bring value to the world. #Awesome is value. And that value includes language. The word "#Awesome" is contagious! I end every meeting with "Create something #Awesome today," which is what I call my podcast as well. We have our own #Awesome alphabet. I built a Facebook mastermind group for my hard-core community. "ABC" is their mantra: always be creating. And the letters don't stop there. Next up, is the triple C: creativity, consistency, and context. I use these to guide me when I'm working on projects. It's my creator philosophy and how I get things done.*

#Family language—Sharon Galor ($$): *We use it all the time, but not in public. I call myself Mama Hen. Only a few key staff members know about it. I love it because it describes that mother figure who everyone relates to. Personal problems? Salsa problems? Mama knows what's best. But every mom needs help. So our studio has volunteer "Helpers." Just like older kids helping out in a #Family. Some helpers graduate to "Instructor" as they progress and are hired on to teach.*

#Extraordinary language—Mark Drager ($$$): *Our language honors our customers. Clients get the #Extraordinary Experience. This really helps people feel it. The name matters, and not just to the customer. It reminds the team to make sure they understand what clients want and are asking for. We're here to help customers grow their business, not ours. We changed the title of the business development director to strategic video consultant because we wanted to focus on the customer.*

#Joy language—Richard Sheridan ($$$$): *We look for ways to inject #Joy through language. Fun language makes the work joyful and that's important. We implement what we call "high-speed voice technology" on the floor. If I want to talk to everyone, I just say, "Hey Menlo!" The place goes quiet and we're in a meeting. Some client projects are confidential, so we come up with code names, like C3PO. Storytelling is core to our culture, so it's no surprise our project management system is based on "story cards." Our language has history. Our name, Menlo Innovations, came from the original Menlo Park, New Jersey, home of Thomas Edison, the man who changed the world by changing a lightbulb.*

#Honest language—Christopher Gavigan ($$$$$): *Simplicity is more #Honest. We discovered that when naming products, it's best to be straightforward. The more we tried fanciful names, the more it confused and alienated our customers. I think of our 125 products as a "portfolio of trust." Safety, health, and performance comes first.*

How do you lead all of this? Do you need policies to enforce your language and your culture?

6. POLICIES

Hell, there are no rules here—we're trying to accomplish something.

—*Thomas A. Edison (American inventor and businessman who developed many devices that influenced life around the world)*

When you have a strong culture based on your One Word, you don't need many strict policies.

BusinessDictionary.com defines "corporate policies" as:

A documented set of broad guidelines, formulated after an analysis of all internal and external factors that can affect a firm's objectives, operations, and plans. Formulated by the firm's board of directors, corporate policy lays down the firm's response to known and knowable situations and circumstances. It also determines the formulation and implementation of strategy, and directs and restricts the plans, decisions, and actions of the firm's officers in achievement of its objectives.

Sounds boring, right?

Because most policies are boring.

Because most companies are boring.

Let me highlight the last part of the statement. It says that corporate policy "directs and restricts the plans, decisions, and actions of the firm's officers."

Your One Word should be directing the plans, decisions, and actions of your team.

Your One Word is your operating philosophy. Every major decision should be run through it. It's the best tool you have to direct your actions, and if your team is using it instead of being restricted by rules, they'll make better, more powerful decisions to help your business grow.

One other section is also worth highlighting: "corporate policy lays down the firm's response to known and knowable situations and circumstances."

The only thing constant about business is that it changes. Using corporate policies to direct your company means you're always playing catch-up. Because it's reactionary. Because it only works with "known and knowable situations," although every single day you have to make decisions based on the unknown.

Policies won't help you be proactive. Your One Word will.

What do #Believe policies look like?

ONE KEY #BELIEVE POLICY

I follow three rules: Do the right thing, do the best you can, and always show people you care.

—*Lou Holtz (former football player, coach, and analyst)*

The most important policy at my business is this: do what you #Believe is right.

To add more context to my rant on the previous page: some policies are helpful. I'm not saying burn them all. There are some known issues for which you can create rules to guide your team, but they shouldn't be the lens through which you operate.

I'd much prefer to hire the right people, people who believe in #Believe, and have them use their judgment instead of limiting them to a set number of actions. Your customers will get a better experience, your team will feel more empowered and happier, and your business will grow.

I used to have lots of policies.

I thought it was the "best practice" thing to do. I had set office hours for my team, specific vacation and sick-day rules, and a bunch of other policies. Then one of my employees had a string of days where he was sick. He'd miss a few hours here, a half day there, and tracking it became a nightmare for me. As he ran out of sick days, he started coming into the office even though he was sick, which wasn't great for me or anyone else on the team. Something seemed broken.

Then I read about Netflix moving to a no-limit vacation policy. I thought it was genius. I immediately implemented it with my staff and everything got better. I stopped having to track sick days. My team stopped coming in when they were sick. And, to my surprise, people took less time off than they did when they were limited.

When you have the right people, you don't need as many policies.

The immediate thought here is, "Well, what if I want to just be on vacation three hundred days per year?" That's not a policy problem. That's a people problem. If your people don't want to come work for you, then you've got a much bigger issue, and forcing them to come in won't solve it.

I applied this thinking across my business.

I got rid of set office hours. I removed the policy of even having to come into the office at all, which eventually led me to selling my office. Slowly I got rid of almost every single traditional policy that you'd expect to find in a business. I put fewer restrictions on my people, and my business grew.

Here are some other One Word policies for you to digest.

ONE WORD POLICY EXAMPLES

If you choose the right people, and you are the right role model for those people, then you don't need a lot of written rules.

—*Sharon Galor ($$)*

#Awesome policies—Roberto Blake ($): *Everyone uses the same tools. My team is virtual. I want us to flow, so our policy is to use the platforms I do. It ensures compatibility in how we're all marketing ourselves. I'll coach if needed, and once we're on the same page, it's easy to create and share #Awesome together. It's a deal breaker if they're not open to operating within our workflow.*

#Family policies—Sharon Galor ($$): *Culture beats policies. We don't have many "official" rules. Sure, I ask my instructors* *to sign a commitment letter, but that's about the extent of anything written. I hire and train the right people for the culture to begin with. We're able to stay #Family oriented because my staff has taken on the ethics and traditions that I personally teach. Our policy is to treat everyone like #Family.*

#Extraordinary policies—Mark Drager ($$$): *We are the least policy-driven company. It's about trust. If you hire the right people in the right culture with the right values, they're not going to take advantage of you. Most of our policies are unspoken truths. For example, a deadline is a deadline. The staff will do whatever it takes to meet one. We don't work just to work. When we go through slow periods, they leave early. If they need to take a day away from the office, they work from home. We don't have a formal vacation policy. We extend them the trust of taking what they need. I trust my team to work when they want—as long as it gets done. If they take advantage, the team will call them on it.*

#Joy policies—Richard Sheridan ($$$$): *Menlo Innovations has very few rules . . . maybe just two! We work on projects in an open environment and we need to be able to hear each other. The first rule is that you can't wear earbuds. The other big rule is that not a single line of code can be written unless we have our partner with us. Other than those two, we have a lot of what you might call "antipolicies." We don't have an in-house HR department. When someone wants to take a day off, they don't have to ask for permission, they simply make a declaration. Every day is "bring your kid to work day." The first baby we brought in was an experiment, and baby Maggie sparked a trend of bringing newborns. Now the team fights over who gets to hold them. We also found that clients interact better with babies around!*

#Honest policies—Christopher Gavigan ($$$$$): *Family makes our office #Honest. The staff is free to bring their kids or their parents. When moms get pregnant, they are able to take as long as they want or come back part-time. We also bring in breakfast or fresh fruits and vegetables from the farmers' markets, free-trade coffee, and sourced water. We provide financial incentives if they drive an electric vehicle. We actually pay them to bring them and charge up at work!*

What if people break the policies? Do they get fired?

7. FIRING

Most people work just hard enough not to get fired and get paid just enough money not to quit.

—*George Carlin (legendary comedian)*

Firing people sucks.

I've never met an entrepreneur who enjoyed firing people, and if you love it you'll probably make a terrible manager of people. You'd like to think that everyone you hire is going to work out and be amazing, but that won't be the case.

The hiring process discussed earlier in this book will help you find better people but you still won't keep everyone.

Just like when you're hiring people, your One Word should help you make the decision when you're firing people.

People who work for you should have two things:

1. The skills needed to complete the responsibilities of the position
2. Alignment with your One Word core value

If they have the alignment but not the skills, you can look at training them or moving them to another position.

If they have the skills but not the alignment, you have a difficult decision to make that remembering your One Word will help clarify.

The classic example is the salesperson, let's call him Jim, who brings in lots of sales but doesn't fit into the culture. Jim is closing accounts every day, but your entire team hates him. So you try to make it work and separate them. Maybe you give Jim an office so he doesn't have to communicate with the rest of the team. After all, Jim is a star salesman. You can't afford to lose him and all the business he brings in, right?

Wrong.

Jim needs to go. And your One Word gives you that clarity to help you make the tough decision. You need people on your team to work together. If they can't work together, then it doesn't work. Everything will slowly crumble until you are forced to make that decision, because the rest of your team is quitting and being unproductive instead of you being proactive about it. Know that there is a Susan out there who has the same skills as Jim, maybe even better skills, *and* fits with the team.

Go find Susan. Now. Here's how I do it around #Believe.

HOW TO FIRE SOMEONE YOU #BELIEVE IN

The best way to fire somebody is to compassionately fire them.
—*Nick Woodman (billionaire CEO of GoPro)*

They say you're supposed to hire slow and fire fast.

I'm pretty good at taking my time to hire the right person

and not just panic hire because I need someone immediately, but I'm not great at firing quickly, even though I've only had to do it once.

It's probably because I #Believe in people, and also hate letting people down, that I always try to find a way to make something work. It's something I'm working on getting better at.

My style of firing is very different from most people.

Fortunately, as mentioned, thanks to my hiring process I've only had to fire one person over the years in my business, but when I did, I never told him he was fired. If someone has to be let go, then obviously they are underperforming and are not happy. I never want to let anyone go who thinks he is killing it and is super-duper happy.

If there's some kind of problem and after multiple conversations with me to try to improve it, he's still not seeing results, he's going to get more and more unhappy. It's up to me to stop the downward spiral.

So my "firing" process is really just sitting down and talking with him. I ask him what he's unhappy with, and if, with all the changes we've tried to make together, this is still a fit for what he wants to do. I tell him I want him to be happy and feel like he has big potential but I don't know how to unlock it here. I ask if he thinks he would be happy somewhere else.

I sit with him and try to brainstorm ideas for what he could do and what other companies he might be able to help. It results in him finally feeling some kind of excitement again—that maybe there is something else out there for him.

So instead of firing him, I help him understand that he could be great and do amazing things, just not with me, so let's figure that out. Let me help you do that. We've kept in touch and he is doing way better and is much happier than when he was with me—which makes me so happy. And I've found a replacement for him who is killing it on my team as well. Everyone wins.

That's #Believe firing. Here are a few more examples.

FIRING AND YOUR ONE WORD

Firing is never fun. Because it's essentially breaking up with someone, and the breakup can be awkward.

—*Christopher Gavigan ($$$$$)*

#Awesome firing—Roberto Blake ($): *#Awesome firing isn't forever. I've ended projects with employees, vendors, sponsors, even clients. Sometimes things just don't work out. It doesn't diminish what we've worked on together. And circumstances might change in the future. Even if I can't move forward with someone at this point in time, it doesn't mean there's not another future possibility. Keep the door open, and keep a friend.*

#Family firing—Sharon Galor ($$): *There's no such thing as firing at Toronto Dance Salsa. The Instructors are independent consultants, so they're not true employees in the first place. So there's not any "firing" in the traditional sense. And, still, I can't remember a time when I've actually fired anyone! I choose people carefully. That's why most of my Instructors stay on for years. If they eventually move on, it's because their life is changing. They're getting married or going back to school, having kids or moving away. If someone's performance isn't up to standards, I'll meet with them to explore how they can be reengaged or motivated to improve.*

#Extraordinary firing—Mark Drager ($$$): *If someone's not a fit, my team's so happy when they walk out the door. I evaluate my staff on four things: quality of work, how they go about the work, whether they are a cultural fit, and whether they provide value for the money. If they aren't performing, the team notices. Every time I've had to let someone go, it came from the staff first. They let me know if a colleague isn't striving to be #Extraordinary. When I fire someone, I consider how it will impact their life. I had someone I planned to fire who was about to buy a house. I let them know right away. I couldn't let them buy a house without knowing.*

#Joy firing—Richard Sheridan ($$$$): *It always starts with the team. My team notices when someone isn't working out and talks to them first. We tell them what's wrong and reset expectations. When offering feedback, they first check in to see if something personal is going on. Maybe their dad is sick or their dog died. And to ask about themselves too: was I my best self? It fosters honest conversations when they consider whether the thing that's wrong with the other person had to do with something they did themselves.*

#Honest firing—Christopher Gavigan ($$$$$): *I want my employees to be #Honestly happy. Sometimes that means that there are people who shouldn't work here, even if they have a passion for our #Honest mission. We prioritize people first, so when someone isn't working out we treat them in a humane way. We give them something they really can work toward. I always give them a chance to improve their work product, by first discussing any issues in a performance evaluation. If it's fairly obvious it's not working out, the employee will usually* *arrive at the separation meeting knowing that it wasn't a good fit. It's generally a mutual decision at that point.*

CHAPTER 6 HIGHLIGHTS

IMPORTANT TAKEAWAYS

- The team you build will make or break your company. Your One Word is the essential ingredient that binds everything together.
- The hiring process is broken. The way most companies hire is insane and extremely ineffective. Hire misfits who are perfect fits for you, and attract them using your One Word.
- If you do a good job hiring, then you shouldn't need to do a lot of onboarding. You've already taken care of it in your hiring process.
- Your environment holds you where you are. If you want to be great, you have to surround yourself with greatness. Does your environment transport you to a different world that people can't wait to come back to?
- Rituals help you design a life with purpose. Rituals are important to business too. They build and reinforce the culture you are creating. They define your business.
- The strongest cultures create their own language. Make your names powerful. Fill them with meaning, and your team will respond accordingly.
- When you have a strong culture based on your One Word you don't need many strict policies. Your One Word should be directing the plans, decisions, and actions of your team.

- Firing people sucks. Just like when you're hiring people, when you're firing people your One Word should help you make the decision. If they have the skills but not the alignment, your One Word will tell you what to do.

COMING UP: *In chapter 7, I'll examine how to run your company operations around your One Word.*

OPERATIONS

Our business is about technology, yes. But it's also about operations and customer relationships.

—Michael Dell (billionaire founder and CEO of Dell Inc.)

This is where we really take it up a notch.

Most people can see how using One Word can help with their marketing campaigns.

Some can see how if you live your One Word they can build a high-performance culture and a workplace where people are proud to join.

The last step is to realize that your One Word isn't just for marketing or culture—it's everything.

Your entire business should be run through the lens of your One Word.

In this chapter we're going to look at how to use your One Word to run the operations of your business through the following areas:

1. Client management
2. Supplier selection
3. Products and services
4. Quality control

5. Research and development
6. Mentors and advisors
7. Raising capital
8. Sales and marketing
9. Project management
10. Tough decisions

Here we go!

1. CLIENT MANAGEMENT

The best way to find yourself is to lose yourself in the service of others.

—*Mahatma Gandhi (preeminent leader of the Indian independence movement in British-ruled India)*

How you treat clients matters.

And it's not enough to just provide great service or follow the Golden Rule.

You need to live your One Word through every interaction with your customers.

Now, hopefully you've used the strategies in the "Campaign" section of this book to attract the customers who share the same core value as you do.

If not, go back and reread it. It's critical to work with ideal clients.

Once you sell something to someone, you've got to manage the relationship.

Maybe the product they bought won't do everything they need. Maybe your service isn't quite getting the results they want. Maybe it's no longer possible to meet the timeline you laid out together at the start.

Some clients will be over-the-moon happy with what you sold them, while others will need reassurance that everything will be okay. Either way, you need to manage the relationship so they get the result they want and can't wait to tell their friends about you.

That's where your One Word comes in.

What happens after I buy from you? Do I get an e-mail? What's in it? Does it reinforce what you stand for?

What if I have a problem with what I bought? Do I call you? What does the person who answers the phone say? How do you fix my issue for me? What kind of follow-up is there afterward to make sure I'm happy?

What do you do to keep in touch with clients after they buy? How do you remain relevant, valuable, and at the top of their mind? Are you giving people something valuable that they'll remember and want to share?

Every single interaction with a client should come from your One Word, and the strategies you use to communicate should also be One Word driven.

I've done it based around #Believe and you can too with your One Word.

#BELIEVE IN YOUR CLIENTS

To give real service you must add something which cannot be bought or measured with money, and that is sincerity and integrity.

—Douglas Adams (bestselling author of The Hitchhiker's Guide to the Galaxy)

#Believe is about making people feel good about themselves, giving them confidence, and helping them reach their goals.

That's what I do for my clients.

For my entrepreneurial clients, I help them set goals, track their progress, connect them with other business owners, promote them on my social channels, do one-on-ones to make sure they are following through, and pick them up when they fall off track.

For my brand-name clients, I give them data about the entrepreneurial world, share advice on how they can improve their marketing campaigns, give them shout-outs on my social media channels, and meet with them to help them brainstorm new ideas.

All of this is on top of what I'm actually being paid to do.

I do it because I #Believe in them, and because I want to see anything that I attach my name to become successful. It's not just about making money. It's about making an impact. If you're around me, you're going to catch some of the #Believe aura and you'll want to do more in your business and your life.

Here's a typical example: One of my entrepreneur clients wanted to share his story on camera but was too afraid of what his friends would think. So the next time he came over I grabbed my video camera, told him I was filming him, guided him through it, and posted it on my YouTube account as well as his Facebook page and tagged his friends (who were all supportive, by the way). He has since gone on to record many videos and has lost his shyness or fear of what others think. He still sees that day as a life-changing moment that helped him and his business grow to new levels.

Another one of my brand clients invited me to speak at an event he was hosting. In passing, one of the client reps mentioned to me that his firm internally set a target of having the conference reach over 100 million impressions on Twitter. I promised that

I'd get them 100 million by myself the next day. I then stayed up until almost 5:00 a.m. scheduling tweets and preparing, despite also having to present onstage later in the afternoon. The next day my scheduled and live tweets totaled 541. At the time I had just over 200,000 followers, giving them over 100 million impressions from my account alone. They were elated.

That's what #Believe client management is all about. But what else can you do?

ONE WORD CLIENT MANAGEMENT

To me it isn't client management; it's client listening and engagement.

—*Christopher Gavigan ($$$$$)*

#Awesome clients—Roberto Blake ($): *Overdelivering for clients is just part of the #Awesome experience. Anyone can hire someone who is great at what they do, but the customer may not like the way that they're required to work with them. I feel that the experience is more important, so I overdeliver on customer service. #Awesome service is about really caring about what you're doing.*

#Family clients—Sharon Galor ($$): *If you treat new customers like new #Family members, that's what they become. It goes way beyond customer service. When you put them first, the chances of them enjoying it and coming back will be very high. I don't want them to come back because I want more money. I just love salsa so much, I can't imagine anyone not wanting to do it. I want to show why I love it so much, to help them feel the same passion for the dance as I do.*

#Extraordinary clients—Mark Drager ($$$): *Great work isn't enough. I want clients to have an #Extraordinary Experience. We're focused on client experience while delivering #Extraordinary work. Here's our process: Understand the ask. Determine what the client is really asking for. Be willing to be ballsy. If clients want #Extraordinary work, they need to be pushed past their comfort zone and do things differently than they are accustomed to. Wow them at every step. We'll even do extra work and eat the costs to make sure we overdeliver. Don't stop until the client is satisfied. I'm hyperfocused on how they will react and manage expectations.*

#Joy clients—Richard Sheridan ($$$$): *#Joy for us means low-tech client communication. We prefer face-to-face conversations with each other and clients. Our clients come in every week for a show-and-tell, to see the work we've completed. Because our tracking is done on handwritten cards, it makes the planning process tangible. It draws the client in. The client can't help but get involved. They'll review and read the cards together with us. The cards have an inscribed box that represents their budget and includes each task and the corresponding time it took. This allows them to visualize and feel how much of their budget has been used. When things take longer or new tasks are needed, the client is in a better position to make those hard decisions on trade-offs.*

#Honest clients—Christopher Gavigan ($$$$$): *It's about #Honest relationships. It's understanding what the client wants out of the relationship. When we listen, we can figure out what they want. I was talking to a mom one late Friday night. She had just put her kids down, and she wanted to talk about our*

Honest wipes. We had a forty-five-minute conversation, and she wanted to know how we made the wipes. She was geeking out about how we built them, where they were sourced, the whole history of developing this product that's become one of the five bestselling wipes in the market.

Now let's find the right suppliers to help you provide great service for your clients.

2. SUPPLIER SELECTION

A smart manager will establish a culture of gratitude. Expand the appreciative attitude to suppliers, vendors, delivery people, and of course, customers.

—*Harvey Mackay (businessman and bestselling author)*

Your suppliers represent your brand.

If the quality of your inputs suffer, your clients will notice and they won't blame your supplier, they'll blame you.

Choosing suppliers is just as important as choosing employees.

It's not just about picking the lowest cost provider.

It's about working with businesses who understand what you stand for and believe in the same thing.

It's about picking suppliers based on your One Word.

The more closely aligned you are, the more they are going to help you grow.

Start with the relationships that mean the most.

You might want the store you buy pens from to be aligned around your One Word, but if you're only going once every six months, then it's not the highest priority on your list.

Where are you spending the most money in your business?

Are the businesses you're spending money with caring for you as much as you care for your clients?

Are they constantly looking for ways you could achieve your goals, even if it has nothing to do with them?

It's a lot easier for people to think of ways to help if they believe in the path that you're on and are on the same one themselves.

Just like customers with big budgets but misaligned values can hurt you . . . Just like employees with the exact skills that you need but who don't fit the culture can hurt you . . . Suppliers who can give you the product or service you need can hurt you if they clash with your One Word.

It's time to start picking suppliers based on what you stand for.

MY SUPPLIERS #BELIEVE

So much business is based on the belief that we should do whatever we can within legal limits to make as much money as we can. Ben & Jerry's was based on values, and we try to operate a business that not just sells ice cream but partners with all our stakeholders— whether that's suppliers or customers—to bring about a more sustainable world.

—Jerry Greenfield (cofounder of Ben & Jerry's)

Let me tell you the story about Ed.

In the early days of my website, I was having a problem with my web hosting. I was getting so much traffic that I kept crashing the servers I was on. A good problem to have, but still a problem. At the time, dedicated servers weren't available, and I kept upgrading to the latest package that the hosting companies provided. It never worked, and my site kept crashing. The Internet is a big part of my business. If my website went down, my business went down. It was beyond frustrating.

Then I met Ed.

As part of my philosophy of giving back, I put on a regular series of workshops to help local entrepreneurs with their search-engine optimization. I called it SEO for Africa, and we raised over $100,000 through the workshops to support entrepreneurs who were starting up in Africa.

Ed was one of my regular attendees.

His business was web hosting. At the time, he was focused on being the most environmentally friendly web-hosting provider in the industry. Now, Ed is a really relaxed guy. He has a surfer dude vibe about him that was very calming but also made me nervous. Could he handle my website? I was going to be his single biggest account and I couldn't afford any more downtime.

But Ed believed in #Believe.

He loved what I was doing and wanted to be a part of it. I knew he actually cared about me and the mission I was on and not just about taking my money, which is way more than I could say for my other web-hosting companies. So I gave him a shot.

And it has been awesome!

We haven't had any downtime since Ed took over. He sends me ideas and updates for what we could do on the server. A year into my contract, he gave me a better configuration that would be 20 percent cheaper. I send him updates on how everything is going and treat him like he's part of the team—because he is.

Now I want all my suppliers to #Believe as much as Ed does.

DO SUPPLIERS BELIEVE IN YOU?

I want to be in vendor relationships where I feel they are more philosophically consistent . . . It matters to me. A lot.
—*Roberto Blake ($)*

#Awesome suppliers—Roberto Blake ($): *I make sure my suppliers are #Awesome. My suppliers are the companies that help me facilitate what I do so I always research them. I review their reputation and take a hard look at the ratings and quality of their products and services. I also look into their employment practices, philanthropy, and environmental impact to see if they match my philosophy.*

#Family suppliers—Sharon Galor ($$): *My suppliers are my customers. Most of my salsa instructors were once customers first! They grew up in our culture and share the same values we do. They'll start by assisting me and then gain more and more teaching time in each class as they progress toward eventually becoming instructors.*

#Extraordinary suppliers—Mark Drager ($$$): *Suppliers are an extension of my company. Fundamentally I would prefer to insource everything because I have such high standards. When someone's working for me, I have the ability to ask the #Extraordinary from them, like coming in at 5:00 a.m. when a project is at deadline. I once did a SWOT analysis that compared us to larger firms. The advice was to lower my risk, as they did, by keeping overhead variable. But I feel that it creates too many inconsistencies, and the cost per project is much higher when you outsource.*

#Joy suppliers—Richard Sheridan ($$$$): *We had our annual holiday party and by tradition we celebrated at Menlo . . . our big, open space is great for big, open parties. There was a lot of cleaning up needed afterward, and we assumed we would come back Monday morning and have some significant cleaning to do. Much to our delight, our cleaning crew went above and beyond and had the place perfectly cleaned for us. That morning, we cheered the cleanliness and one of our programmers suggested a collection as a thank-you for the cleaning crew, and within a few minutes had raised three hundred dollars from the team. Joy!*

#Honest suppliers—Christopher Gavigan ($$$$$): *Suppliers have to share our #Honest passion. We are ridiculously rigorous in our selection standards. As rigid and strong as our requests and demands are, we've made mistakes and chosen suppliers that aren't as knowledgeable or passionate about our values. Fair-labor practices are a key element of our requirements. We do a big audit on our suppliers' labor practices. We look at how far away the labor is done, because that makes a huge ecological impact. And we consider what is happening where that labor is occurring. We've got to dig deep and do a tremendous amount of education. We also look at their environmental footprint and sustainability efforts. We examine the content of what they're supplying to us. A lot of the raw ingredients we source will come with their own proportion of preservatives. Unlike some of our competitors, we factor that into our final product, and are transparent about that with our consumers. Part of our job of being #Honest is to bring up the standards. It's a win if someone copies us and elevates the entire marketplace.*

You have your suppliers. Now it's time to create products and services that matter.

3. PRODUCTS AND SERVICES

When Henry Ford made cheap, reliable cars people said, "Nah, what's wrong with a horse?" That was a huge bet he made, and it worked.

—*Elon Musk (billionaire CEO of Tesla Motors and SpaceX)*

Elon Musk wants to colonize Mars.

Not just send a rocket to Mars. He wants people to *live* on Mars. That dream is not physically possible given our current science and technology. Musk needs to cut the cost to reach space by a factor of ten. He needs to create reusable launch vehicles. He needs to design products that have never been designed before.

The way most businesses choose new products and services is flawed.

You look at the data, you do the market research, you compare prices, you analyze the costs, you see if you can make a profit, and if you can then you launch. That's only half the equation. This is classic "acting with the head" decision making and will always limit the impact that you can have.

You need to make big decisions with your heart and the little ones with your head.

Your product-and-service decision should start with your One Word. What's the positive change you want to make in the world and how can the products or services you create contribute to that vision? Elon Musk is using his vision of colonizing Mars to guide the production process to create whatever needs to be created to realize his dream. Let your heart guide your big decisions, then use your head to figure out how to do it.

Let me show you how I create around #Believe.

#BELIEVEWORTHY PRODUCTS

I strongly believe that missionaries make better products. They care more . . . it's not just about the business.

—*Jeff Bezos (billionaire founder of Amazon.com)*

Making money is never the first thing when I launch a new product or service.

Making an impact is. And when you make an impact, you can make money.

I #Believe in entrepreneurs and want to help one billion business owners. That's the mission I'm on, and every product or service decision I make is tied to achieving that goal.

Let's take my YouTube channel as an example.

I'm all-in on YouTube at the time of this writing. I love recording videos for my audience. My skills lend themselves well to video over other mediums. I'm a visual learner as well and I love being able to teach people in a way that reaches them. I pick topics for my videos that I'm passionate about—things I wish I had when I was starting my business or even things I wish were available right now. Videos that are needed that nobody else is creating, that I wish were created—so I create them.

That's the heart.

I post to YouTube because it's the biggest video platform. If that changes, I'll change. I optimize titles, add descriptions, create playlists, put in tags—because that helps the videos rank well.

That's the head.

You need both, but the decision is made with the heart and the "how" to accomplish it is figured with the head.

Let's say we flipped it.

Let's say I start with the head and am just trying to make money, so I go to YouTube because it's popular. I look at some of the most viewed videos and see they're songs, cute cats, and fail videos. So I try to make songs, cute-cat videos, and fail videos. But I'll never make it. Because I don't care about cute cats. So I won't put the effort needed into making the best cute-cat videos available online. And so I lose. Sure I might make a few bucks, but I'll never strike it rich or have a huge impact.

Big decisions with your heart, small ones with your head—always.

CREATING AROUND YOUR HEART

> Clients come to us for what they want, and we work really hard to give them what we want to give them.
> —Mark Drager ($$$)

#Awesome creations—Roberto Blake ($): *I focus on the areas of my business that make the most impact. I examine the analytics of my YouTube channel to evaluate which videos and playlists are performing better. I measure which ones get the most response, and what the content is. Then I can make more or less content around specific areas. Passion is a big metric for me. I don't just look at the numbers; I look at my tribe's response. I carefully survey the comments to see which topics are being talked about. I'm constantly doing projections of the monetary ROI I'll get from each of my projects. But the ROI doesn't always have to be monetary. It just has to advance my personal mantra.*

Creating #Awesome is about spreading inspiration for myself and my tribe.

#Family creations—Sharon Galor ($$): *Our #Family determines which type of classes we teach. We look at what new classes students are asking for. Salsa is our base, but we get waves of interest in other styles besides salsa. Classes like tango, West Coast swing, and the jive come in and out of trend, so we pay attention and teach the classes when our #Family asks for them.*

#Extraordinary creations—Mark Drager ($$$): *My expectations for our work are usually much higher than our clients'. There's a constant balance between what my clients want, and how we want to give them something even more #Extraordinary. Clients don't always understand the work that goes into a project, so they might not know when they're being taken advantage of by another company that's bidding against us.*

#Joy creations—Richard Sheridan ($$$$): *#Joy is the product we sell. Companies hire us to develop something specific for them, but we place the priority on adding great value to their end users. Essentially they are agreeing, "Yes, we want to thrill our consumers" too. The projects we are pulled into are the ones where people believe that our culture of #Joy will ultimately add value to their bottom line.*

#Honest creations—Christopher Gavigan ($$$$$): *We only make products if our #Honest perspectives on health and design are met. It has to be safe and nontoxic for you and your family. If it's even remotely possible to have a negative impact, then we won't use it. We're bringing innovation into the market, but we* *won't sacrifice health. Beautiful design is part of our brand, so the product must be artfully crafted. We aim to be unpretentious about it, to stay on the side of clean and natural. It has to perform well and be priced as accessibly as possible. We might need to shrink our margins so we can stay in that sweet spot for the end user. They might have to pay a little more, but know it's high quality, lasts longer, and is better for the earth. If it's made with good intention and purpose, and it works, people will buy it.*

Okay, now your product is great. How can you maintain the quality as you grow?

4. QUALITY CONTROL

Be a yardstick of quality. Some people aren't used to an environment where excellence is expected.

—*Steve Jobs (billionaire entrepreneur and cofounder of Apple Computer)*

You need to be proud of the products and services you create.

Would you show what you made to your mother? Would you recommend that your husband or wife use what you're selling? Are you looking forward to showing your grandchildren what you did and telling them, "I made this!"

Everything you create has to have your stamp of approval on it.

This is your legacy that you're building.

This is what people are going to remember you for.

Make it count.

Your One Word should ooze out of the product and/or service you create.

If your offering doesn't make someone feel #Believe or #Calm or #Family or whatever your One Word is, then your quality control failed.

Your One Word is the lens through which you see the world and operate your company. It's your compass that tells you the right direction to go.

Most quality control processes follow a checklist.

- Does it weigh what it's supposed to weigh?
- Does it meet the industry guidelines that we are required to follow?
- Does it have spelling or grammar mistakes?
- Does it match what our client asked us to create?
- Does it pass customer satisfaction surveys?
- Etc., etc., etc.

All great points but missing the most important quality check of all:

Does it make people feel our One Word?

Because if it doesn't, you're sunk.

You might close a few sales, but you're not going to get people to care.

If you want people to care about your products, you need to show you care about them and believe in them first.

QUALITY TO #BELIEVE IN

The quality of a leader is reflected in the standards they set for themselves.

—*Ray Kroc (built McDonald's and his family fortune is worth billions of dollars)*

There was the time 50 Cent called one of my YouTube videos "Good sh*t."

Three days before he did, I was about to cancel the video's release. Here's what happened: I tasked my team with making a video about 50 Cent and the advice that entrepreneurs could learn from his success. Two people on my team put five hours of research into it, double what we normally spend, and sent it to me. The only problem was it wasn't good enough.

It was good, but it wasn't #Believe good.

Sure, people would watch it because it was 50 Cent's name, but would it inspire people? Would it change people's lives? Would it have an impact? I didn't think so. It was past dinnertime, and the video needed to be finished that night so my editor could put it all together. So I spent the next three hours fixing it, making it #Believe quality. I was tired, annoyed, and frustrated at having to jump in at the last minute to fix it, but I was proud of the end product and got it out to meet our deadline.

50 Cent liked it too.

Someone found it and showed it to him. He then shared it on his blog, to his Twitter and Facebook feeds, and he sent the video to over fifty thousand views in twenty-four hours. Would he have done that if we released the original version? Maybe, but probably not. Busy people don't usually get into the habit of sharing "just okay" things. People share what makes an impact on them. Did I know 50 Cent was going to share it? Of course not—but I wasn't surprised either that someone would send it to him.

Because I wouldn't let the video get released until I stood by #Believe quality.

STANDING BY YOUR ONE WORD

Having me as the one training everyone is the biggest way I've found to keep our quality high.

—*Sharon Galor ($$)*

#Awesome quality—Roberto Blake ($): *I am the judge and jury for my own work product. Without my own regular full-time staff, I have to hold myself accountable to keeping high-quality content. I rely on the three Cs (creativity, consistency, and context) to help me evaluate whether and how I'm creating something #Awesome. If something is less than #Awesome, people also let me know. My own tribe helps keep me accountable for producing great work. Because I produce and share such a large volume of content with the public, the feedback I get is a great gauge. This is true for my client work too. If the work on my website or in my portfolio isn't drawing in new business, I know it needs to get better.*

#Family quality—Sharon Galor ($$): *Everyone has to be trained through me. Making sure that I'm the one person teaching our Instructors is the best way to keep our class structure consistent. Even very experienced Instructors still need to be trained by me, so they get a true sense of the #Family culture. As Mama Hen, I make sure the instructors are taking care of everyone in the #Family.*

#Extraordinary quality—Mark Drager ($$$): *I hire people who are better at the task than I am. My team often has higher standards for the work than I do! They're going to go above and beyond to create a high-quality product they are proud of. I trust that things get done well because my team will* *naturally fight hard to be #Extraordinary. Our process allows for better results. There's a flexibility built into our methodical process, so if we make a mistake it's easy to pivot. When a video is produced, there are roughly twenty check-ins with the client.*

#Joy quality—Richard Sheridan ($$$$): *Because our programmers work in pairs, we work together to problem solve. If you're familiar with Six Sigma, they call it moving source and inspection together. You catch errors sooner because two people are working next to each other. Someone is always watching and paying close attention. Because we switch partners every five days, a new partner will come in and review and ask questions about why the pair from the previous week used certain code. This leads to alerting their new partner why that might not work. And the partner from last week is just across the table, throwing in his opinion too.*

#Honest quality—Christopher Gavigan ($$$$$): *We do quality checks every step of the way. We hire a lot of third-party auditors to help us check our work, as well as utilizing distinctly separate internal departments to audit across production. The shipping and billing is done out of our own warehouse. When product comes in, it goes to quarantine. After it passes quality check with our third-party audit, as well as through our internal set of procedures, then it can be put into inventory.*

Your products are rocking. But how do you create a consistent lineup of winners?

5. RESEARCH AND DEVELOPMENT

Innovation has nothing to do with how many R&D dollars you have...It's not about money. It's about the people you have, how you're led, and how much you get it.

—*Steve Jobs (billionaire entrepreneur and cofounder of Apple Computer)*

Research and development helps you accomplish your impossible goals.

If you want people to care about your business, you need to be on a powerful mission. Your One Word will guide that mission and your products and services will reflect it.

Your vision for the world should surpass the limitations of current solutions, and to make real progress you need to invest in your products, technology, and people so they can do what others feel cannot be done.

The first step is to align your team.

People need to understand the "why" of what they're working on before they get started on the "how."

As an entrepreneur you get to see the reactions to what you create. You get to deal with customers and see the happy looks on their faces. You get to understand the real impact you're having on people's lives when they tell you how much of a difference you've made.

That's fuel for you to keep going.

Most of your people are behind the scenes and never get to see those results. Sure, they get the satisfaction from knowing they hit their target, that they created something that has never been created, and from knowing that they completed a project—and there's a great feeling of accomplishment in that.

But it's not the same.

If you can show people that the work they are doing is changing lives, they'll give you, not just their minds, but their hearts and souls as well.

It starts with your mindset. You need an important "why" that aligns with your One Word and will inspire people to come work for you. Then you need to be on a big mission that surpasses what is currently possible. And then you need to empower your people to give it everything they have by showing the impact their work will have on the lives of real people.

You need your people to #Believe in what they're creating for you.

#BELIEVE R&D

> You have to have a big vision and take very small steps to get there. You have to be humble as you execute but visionary and gigantic in terms of your aspiration.
> —*Jason Calacanis (Internet entrepreneur, blogger, and angel investor)*

My best ideas come from me, my team, and my customers.

You will always be a great source of ideas. It's your baby, and you have the passion and drive to push your business forward. How well your team and customers come up with new ways to help you accomplish your big goals will depend on how well you articulate your One Word, the meaning behind it, and the impact it's having.

I'm very fortunate.

Every day I get to wake up to hundreds of positive e-mails, YouTube comments, and posts across my social channels, thanking me for the work I'm doing. It's an amazing feeling knowing that I'm helping people, and I love starting my day with it.

But what about my team? People love my YouTube videos and thank me, but what about Jason who helps me film them, Ivan and Nina who help me research them, Jani and Steve and J-Ryze who help train me to be better, and Christina and Sam who help edit them? And what about all the people who are behind all the other projects I'm working on? How do they stay inspired and get ideas to help us reach more people?

The answer is to share.

Every Monday morning I find stories people have shared with me and I send them to the team. I thank them for their work and for being a part of this important business. I let them know that I couldn't do it without them. Hearts and souls. I also update everyone on the important projects I'm working on. Everyone gets an update because you never know where great ideas will come from. I might be working on my YouTube channel and my programmer comes up with a new idea. You wouldn't expect that since there is no coding involved in my videos, but if I didn't let him know what we were doing, I would have never have received his input.

Then there are customers.

I let everyone know what I'm doing, from big customers who pay me hundreds of thousands of dollars to a YouTube subscriber who hasn't paid me a dime. I let them know what I'm doing, show them why it's important, and ask for their feedback. They're often the source behind some of my best research and development ideas. They care about helping me because they know I care about them.

The answer for me is to #Believe in myself, my team, and my customers.

YOUR ONE WORD R&D ANSWERS

As soon as we heard about the Kizomba craze, we researched who the best instructors were, where we could get them, and a few weeks later we were offering a Kizomba class.

—*Sharon Galor ($$)*

#Awesome R&D—Roberto Blake ($): *#Awesome R&D usually only requires my time. When I've determined I have the skills required to build something out, I save myself a lot of money by doing it myself. Most companies need to allocate a large budget for R&D. Fortunately, for the most part, I haven't had to do this. I find that solopreneurs like myself will tend to find a way to make time to learn how to do it themselves. I always believe in being a practitioner first.*

#Family R&D—Sharon Galor ($$): *At the end of every semester we ask our students to weigh in on our classes. Their input makes our company evolve. When a new dance style becomes popular, like with Kizomba recently, we quickly research the style and our options. We'll reach out to different instructors, and within a few weeks we can have a new class running . . . because it's what our #Family wants.*

#Extraordinary R&D—Mark Drager ($$$): *Being #Extraordinary means keeping focused on video trends in the marketplace. We'll pay attention to what style of videos are being produced in a specific industry to see where there is demand. Graphic videos had grown in popularity, so I determined we should start doing more of this type of work. We looked at* *examples of other high-profile work to see what we'd like to do. We got so good at it, we started winning awards. This created a new niche for us so that we could more easily repeat and focus on ways to sell it again and again.*

#Joy R&D—Richard Sheridan ($$$$): *The five-day cycle of adjustment is central to our R&D here. We do five days of discovery and five days of development, and then do it all over again. Our clients help us on both sides of the process too. And, really, almost everything we do is client driven, as their projects lead to finding solutions that may not exist yet. Some would say it's more profitable to build a widget and sell it over and over, but we think that's too simplistic. We'll also trade away design work for shares in our clients' companies. They do all the market research and product marketing, so we know we're building something where there's a burning passion.*

#Honest R&D—Christopher Gavigan ($$$$$): *The Honest Company sets the standards. Our job is to stay abreast of the latest science, medicine, academia, and formulation science and toxicology to understand how certain chemicals and ingredients are impacting the environment and, ultimately, human health. If something is shown in data to be linked to disease or irritation, or decreases human health in any way, our job to take a precautionary approach. It's better to be safe than sorry, and not use it. We create our own standards for the marketplace. #Honest R&D sets the practical standards for the marketplace to follow.*

You've got all the ingredients for a great business. But who do you turn to for advice?

6. MENTORS AND ADVISORS

> One of the best pieces of advice I ever got was from a horse master. He told me to go slow to go fast. I think that applies to everything in life. We live as though there aren't enough hours in the day but if we do each thing calmly and carefully we will get it done quicker and with much less stress.
>
> —*Viggo Mortensen (Oscar-nominated actor and artist)*

The people you surround yourself with matter.

You don't have all the answers and you can't do this alone. Any great undertaking involves the minds, efforts, and hearts of multiple people. If you try to do everything yourself, you will never reach your full potential because your blind spots and weaknesses will hold you and your business back.

Just like hiring the right employees matter, so does choosing the right advisors to guide you. And like every other big decision, it all starts with your One Word. You need to know who they are and what they stand for before you worry about the skills or knowledge that they bring. If you don't share the same values, then you're going to clash. They may seem like a perfect fit in terms of their experience and connections, but that difference could sink your business.

Advisors are there to push you.

They are advisors for a reason. They know something about something that you don't, and they want to help you. They should believe in you and stretch your comfort zone. They should help mold you to be a more complete entrepreneur. Making you feel uncomfortable because they're pushing you to learn a new skill or test your limiting self-beliefs is natural and healthy. Making you feel uncomfortable because they want you to do something that's not aligned with your One Word is not.

When you're clear about what you stand for, you'll attract advisors who love you.

Just like skilled employees, skilled advisors have lots of options. They can go to any company. Why are they going to come to you? What makes you so different? Why would they choose you even if you couldn't pay them as much, or anything, compared to other businesses?

The answer is your One Word.

The answer is because you stand for something. The answer is because you're doing something important. The answer is because you're trying to change the world in a positive way. So lead with it. Make people feel it. And you'll start to attract like-minded people.

You need an advisory team that helps you #Believe.

#BELIEVEWORTHY ADVISORS

Colleagues are a wonderful thing—but mentors, that's where the real work gets done.

—*Junot Díaz (Pulitzer Prize–winning author and creative writing professor at MIT)*

I didn't have any business mentors growing up.

My parents were great personal mentors for me. They instilled a lot of the values in me that I hold true today. They helped shape who am I as an individual, and I'm forever grateful for that. But I never really had any business mentors. I didn't have an Uncle Joe entrepreneur I looked up to and wanted to be like. In my high school yearbook where they ask you where you see yourself in ten years, I said I'd be a VP at a bank.

When I started as an entrepreneur and was struggling, I

realized I needed help so I went to the bank. I didn't know anybody else and figured banks were there to help entrepreneurs, right?

Then I discovered aspirational mentors.

Aspirational mentors are people who you look up to and learn from. They are people you've never met but might one day. Some of them might be dead, but you can still learn from their success.

A. P. Giannini taught me to support and believe in the underdog. Donald Trump taught me to think bigger. Steve Jobs taught me to do work that matters. Howard Schultz taught me to stand up for what I believe in. Kanye West taught me not to box myself in. Bill Gates taught me to form alliance partnerships. Warren Buffett taught me to build a moat around my business. Martha Stewart taught me to create a personal brand. Mark Cuban taught me to outwork my competition. Tim Ferriss taught me how to be more productive. Oprah Winfrey taught me to have more heart. Steve Wozniak taught me to create for myself—and so on.

I've never personally had a conversation with any of these people (yet), but through videos, articles, books, and interviews I've learned how to be a more successful entrepreneur.

I've been fortunate to have some real-life mentors that I've been able to directly ask help from. I've also had a couple of amazing mastermind groups that push me to be better and help me bounce ideas around.

But the most significant advisors I've ever had for my business are people I don't have a personal connection to. You can do the same.

Go get some aspirational mentors of your own.

BONUS: MY FAV ENTREPRENEUR

Serving the needs of others is the only legitimate business today.

—A. P. Giannini (founder of Bank of America)

My favorite entrepreneur is Bank of America founder A. P. Giannini.

Wait . . . a banker?

Yep! But he's no ordinary banker. He was the #Believe banker.

The way he built and grew his company serves as a constant inspiration for me and what I'm building right now. Even though he died over sixty-five years ago, his path to success can still be modeled and applied today.

The son of recent immigrants from Genoa, Italy, Giannini left school at fourteen to work at his stepfather's produce store. For the next five years, Giannini devoted himself to the store. He took on the job of public relations, writing letters to all their potential clients and suppliers, and following up in person.

When he was nineteen years old, Giannini's stepfather rewarded his hard work by making him a partner in the thriving business. When he was thirty-two, after becoming a pillar of the community around him, Giannini decided to sell his share in the business to look for a new challenge.

He quickly began receiving offers from other businesses eager to snap him up, but there was one in particular that caught his attention: the Columbus Savings & Loan Association asked Giannini to join its board of directors.

The Columbus S&L was a modest bank headquartered in the Italian section of North Beach. Giannini decided to accept the offer, in the hopes that the position would allow him to both hold a prestigious title and to help society.

For the next two years, Giannini devoted himself to the bank, and things seemed to be progressing smoothly—that is, until he began to encounter difficulties with the bank's other directors.

Giannini wanted to help hardworking immigrants like his parents.

But the Columbus S&L had little interest in extending loans to anyone except businessmen and people who were already wealthy.

In other words, you could only get money if you already had some money.

This didn't make sense to Giannini. Because he #Believed in people.

However, his pleas to lend to the working class fell on deaf ears.

Giannini decided he would do something about it.

THE #BELIEVE BANKER STEPS UP

A banker should consider himself a servant of the people, a servant of the community.

—A.P. Giannini (founder of Bank of America)

It was time to do the right thing and stand up for people.

In 1904, Giannini raised $150,000 from his stepfather and ten other friends, and opened the Bank of Italy. The Bank of Italy was located in a converted saloon right across the street from the Columbus S&L; even the saloon's bartender was kept on, in the role of assistant teller. It might not have been the most professional of ventures—he solicited business door-to-door at a time when doing so was considered unethical—but that didn't matter.

The Bank of Italy allowed Giannini to fulfill his dream of

helping the working class. Within one year, deposits to this "bank for the little guy" exceeded $700,000.

By 1906, deposits to the Bank of Italy had surpassed $1 million. Giannini seemed to be on top of the world—and then disaster struck.

On April 18, 1906, San Francisco was hit by one of the largest earthquakes in its history; much of the city was destroyed. Where other banks took as long as one month to reopen, Giannini reopened the Bank of Italy in just six days. He may have been operating from just a plank stretched across two barrels in the street, but for those who needed loans—and now more than ever—the fact that he was operating at all was enough. Giannini would make loans to people based on a handshake and "a look in their eye."

Can you imagine a banker giving someone a loan today after a handshake and a look in their eye?

Giannini bet on a young entrepreneur named Walt Disney when nobody else would. He bet on financing the Golden Gate Bridge when nobody else would.

That's a #Believe banker.

The biggest lesson I've learned from A. P. Giannini is to fight for the little guy.

I have made it my mission to help entrepreneurs and to believe in them when nobody else does.

Giannini stood up to harsh critics, and everything he did was with the entrepreneur in mind. This serves as a constant reminder for me in deciding how I run my business.

Find the A. P. Giannini who inspires you, and he or she will impact your business just like he did mine.

Now let's look at how some other One Word entrepreneurs find their mentors.

ONE WORD MENTOR EXAMPLES

You can stalk someone on the Internet, and extrapolate from them. Someone like Gary Vaynerchuk, for example, who is the Grand Poo-Bah of Hustling, because he puts out a lot that we can consume.

—*Roberto Blake ($)*

#Awesome mentors—Roberto Blake ($): *I've formed a mastermind group as my effectual board of advisors. The Always Be Creating #Awesome mastermind group is composed of a general paid membership who can network and collaborate on their creative businesses with each other. The group has limited seating. If creative solopreneurs want to join, there is an application and interview process. I'm looking to see if they can create value for others in the group and that they will share as well as take advice and feedback. I both get and give #Awesome guidance there.*

#Family mentors—Sharon Galor ($$): *I don't have a board, so I go to my #Family for advice. Everyone I talk to is within the #Family; my Instructors, Administrators, Helpers, and students. For example, the person who redid our website was one of our Helpers. He knew our environment and our #Family values. He had been with us for a couple of years and started out as a student. He was excited about helping us, and he made us a really nice website! The person who took the photos for the website was also a student and an amateur photographer on the side. I keep it in the #Family.*

#Extraordinary mentors—Mark Drager ($$$): *A few key advisory groups have been very important to my success: Peer* *mentorship, or "mastermind," is a formal group of people who are in similar or larger businesses in all different industries. Business coaching helped me when I first got going. I knew how to make videos, but not how to build a business. Mentor lunches: I schedule lunches with people I aspire to be like. They share invaluable information—maybe they see a younger version of themselves in me. Client lunches: talking to clients is also a fantastic way to learn about how to do business.*

#Joy mentors—Richard Sheridan ($$$$): *Everybody who comes through our doors wants us to be here another day. They don't just want us to survive; they want us to thrive and grow. Because of our openness to let people come in and see what we're doing, there are a whole bunch of people who would simply not allow us to shut down Menlo and #Joy. They would come here in their robes and slippers at 3:00 a.m. if they needed to.*

#Honest mentors—Christopher Gavigan ($$$$$): *Board engagement and selection is so, so important. I'm a firm believer that you should have people around you who will equal parts support and challenge you. I see our board in the same way. They both help and guide, as well as poke and push. Some people might shy away from someone who might give friction, but I like an appropriate discomfort. It makes us better. Yes, profit margin is essential, and you need that. But they know that our mission and social view is long term. Everyone on the board rallies around that.*

Can your mentors and your One Word help you raise capital too?

7. RAISING CAPITAL

> An entrepreneur needs to know what they need, period. Then they need to find an investor who can build off whatever their weaknesses are—whether that's through money, strategic partnerships, or knowledge.
>
> —Daymond John (founder of FUBU and investor on Shark Tank)

You don't want just anybody's money.

Raising money is like hiring a team in that you want people who don't just have the resources you need but also believe in what you're doing.

Many entrepreneurs are so desperate for investment that they don't care who gives it to them—as long as they get it!

Don't be that person.

That's like being so desperate to have a child that you'll insta-marry someone without regard to how you're actually going to live together or raise the child.

Investors are people too, and they come with their own sets of skills, connections, resources, and values.

Bringing money isn't enough. The ideal investor should bring you everything: Capital. Connections. Ideas. Resources. And a shared set of values.

Just as your One Word can be the honey to attract the right customers and employees, it will also help you bring in the best investors.

When you're out raising capital, you're one of many companies with similar ideas. When I was in the venture capital business, I was shocked at how many people had similar ideas and pitches. You think your idea is unique—but it's really not. That's why investors don't sign nondisclosure agreements—they just see too many similar companies.

So how do you stand out?

Use your One Word. Put your purpose front and center. People will love it or they'll hate it, and, again, that's great! Because the person who hates your One Word is never going to be a good investor for you. You'll never get along well and it's better for them to self-eliminate now. And for the people who love it, you've now given them a clear indication of how you *are* unique compared to all the other business plans they are seeing.

If you want to get the right investor to give your business your best shot at funding success, lead with your One Word.

FUNDING #BELIEVE

When people are genuinely happy at the successes of others, the pie gets larger.

—*Stephen Covey (educator, businessman, keynote speaker, and author of* The Seven Habits of Highly Effective People)

I've never had to raise money for my businesses.

Despite coming from a venture capital background, I've never gone out and raised money because I personally don't believe in spending money before I'm making it. I believe that's the best way to build a business and to ensure that you're not making too many expensive mistakes. Try. Fail. Try again. Fail. Keep trying until you hit on a winner. Fail fast. Fail often. And fail cheaply.

I have a creative way of raising capital—I bet on people.

What do you need money for? In most businesses, it's people. You don't need an office or business cards or a company truck or even a website to start. But if you want to scale, you will need people.

So I identify top people and give them a cut.

Instead of raising money to pay for salaries, I'll look at specific opportunities within my business and look for ways to partner with someone. I might pay a small salary or no salary at all. They get paid as they develop that part of the business. The more it grows, the more they get paid.

Sure, it might cost me more in the long run. Why would I give up 10–50 percent of revenue on a project when I could just raise money or invest my own and pay a salary?

That's easy.

First, my downside is limited. If the person doesn't perform, then I'm not out a ton of cash. So many entrepreneurs focus only on the upside and forget to protect their downside. I'd much rather have 50–90 percent of a big success with very little downside than 100 percent of something that has a lot of risk.

Second, I want people invested in the project. I want people to feel like they have ownership—that they have the ability to control their future. That they can make important decisions and if they work harder and get results, they'll be rewarded.

Not everyone enjoys this kind of opportunity. Many people prefer just having a salary that they can depend on. And that's cool too. It's about understanding your people and where they want to go.

Instead of raising capital, I love to #Believe in people and build the business together.

RAISING ONE WORD MONEY

If you can rally people around your core concepts, you can find alignment.

—*Christopher Gavigan ($$$$$)*

#Awesome money—Roberto Blake ($): *I've got multiple #Awesome pipelines for building revenue. In addition to website* *design, I work as a writer, video marketer, and consultant. I've developed other income streams too, such as affiliate marketing and YouTube. A big fat check from an investor isn't interesting to me. Because of my diversity of revenue and low overhead, I'm on track to scale my business on my own. I've been able to be self-sustainable with the #Awesome value I create.*

#Family money—Sharon Galor ($$): *I never raised additional money; I worked within my budget. I started by renting space hourly from gyms. I would pay thirty dollars per hour, with students paying me ten dollars per hour for a class. I added more classes and then locations. I lived within my means and put extra revenue toward expanding classes. It wasn't until several years later, when I had a regular stream of students, that I signed a lease on a studio. I was very safe. I didn't want to overextend myself, so I never borrowed money. It was important that it didn't become an impersonal school, so I expanded slowly and made sure the quality, service, and #Family didn't suffer.*

#Extraordinary money—Mark Drager ($$$): *Being #Extraordinary means staying lean, mean, and hungry. I've intentionally slowed growth so I can stay in that sweet spot of not having to go into debt to scale. I've been accused of being overgenerous with my salaries, but superlean on everything else. But I've found that when I pay well, I don't need to hire as many people because my team does better work more quickly. Staying lean allows us all to keep pushing to be #Extraordinary.*

#Joy money—Richard Sheridan ($$$$): *We've never had to raise capital. Each of the founders wrote a fifteen-thousand-dollar check on day one and never had to write another. I didn't bring a salary home during the first six months. There were lean* *years, especially with 9/11 and the recession in 2008. We decided early on that we didn't want to take outside money. We might have been able to grow faster if we had. But we didn't want to kowtow to people who may not have cared about Menlo and #Joy as much as we do, so we purposely chose not to take investment capital that might risk our mission. We stayed in control of our destiny.*

#Honest money—Christopher Gavigan ($$$$$): *In the early days it was just me and Jessica with a vision and a dream. But we couldn't self-fund for much longer. A business like ours needed to be infused with capital. It was important to us to have enough capital that we had room to maneuver and pivot, while staying visionary. We initially raised $7 million. To date we've raised more than $227 million. What's interesting is that over 80 percent of that still sits on balance sheets today. We're not looking to buy growth. We are very measured in how we build the business. We're very mindful about how we spend the money and who we raise money from.*

If you raise money, where should it be spent? Is it worth hiring a sales force?

8. SALES AND MARKETING

Word of mouth is the most valuable form of marketing, but you can't buy it. You can only deliver it. And you have to really deliver.

—G-Eazy *(rapper, songwriter, and record producer)*

This section is going to upset a lot of people.

You don't need to have a sales force to be successful in business.

There . . . I said it.

Now, you do need people to answer calls, help customers, project manage, and so forth, but you don't need to have salespeople doing outbound sales.

What you do need is to get attention.

We're all in the attention business. The more attention we get, the more we can sell, and the way to get attention isn't to spam people, cold-call them, knock on their door, and harass them.

Standing for something important gets people's attention. Doing something that matters gets people's attention. Building a unique company and culture gets people's attention. It helps you rise above the noise.

Instead of leaving an endless stream of voice mails that people never respond to, how about actually giving your customers an experience and a message that is worth talking about?

Instead of trying to convince me that you have the best product or service for me, how about you kick up so much noise in your industry because of what you stand for that I come to you asking how we might work together?

The traditional salesperson needs to evolve . . . or they will die.

Your company needs storytellers—people who will spread your message and impact the community. You need people who care about the mission of the business and put that before meeting their sales quota. You need people who have the courage to do something that is outside the comfort zone and beyond the expectations of most people.

That's how you create awareness. That's how you get people coming to you and talking about you. That's how you sell.

And it all starts with your One Word.

BELIEVE SELLING

Transforming a brand into a socially responsible leader doesn't happen overnight by simply writing new marketing and advertising strategies. It takes effort to identify a vision that your customers will find credible and aligned with their values.

—*Simon Mainwaring (branding consultant, creative director, and social media specialist)*

"I don't get it, Evan. What is your business model? How do you make money?"

I recently acquired a new business and brought in a director of operations to run and grow it. He knows me more as a friend than from the business world, and he was confused and amazed at what I did for a living, so he asked me about it.

I explained to him that my business model is kicking up as much noise as possible in my industry and monetizing that attention. He either thought I was going off the deep end or being way too philosophical, but that's the truth of my business and how I make money from it.

Just like you, I'm in the attention game.

Everything I do is about increasing the impact I have. One, because it makes me feel good. It nourishes my soul to help people. And, two, because it makes more money. The more attention I create, the more money I will make.

That's why almost everything I do has to be at scale. I make YouTube videos because I can have a massive reach. I'm active on Twitter because I can access many people. I wrote this book because it could have a big impact. If what I'm working on is not going to have the possibility of having a real impact on many people's lives, then I'm usually not interested.

I kick up a lot of dust and then monetize it.

Most of what I do is actually free. The videos, the content, the interactions—most of it I don't get paid to do. And that's what gives me incredible leverage. As a result of just doing what I love and helping people, I've built an amazing #BelieveNation community and opportunities (like this book!) just come to me. The bigger my community is, the more opportunities I get.

And I don't do any outbound selling. Zero.

Beyond that, I also don't follow up with anybody. If you ask for a quote and I don't hear back from you, I'm not following up. Rather than try to convince you to buy, I'm going to spend time on clients who are already converted and then kick up more noise so you keep hearing my name.

That's #Believe sales and marketing. :)

SELLING YOUR ONE WORD

We have no PR company, no PR team. I go to PR conferences and people ask how we did it. I tell them that they don't want to know. They'll get fired.

—*Richard Sheridan ($$$$)*

#Awesome selling—Roberto Blake ($): *I use social media to invite a conversation. I usually start by telling someone I think my audience would love what they're doing, and why. It works great because I'm usually already engaged with their brand by then, and have already shared what I like about them to my tribe. I do absolutely zero cold-calling, but I might cold-tweet! My practice of tweeting out my content has been very successful in generating relationships. I've generated relationships with C-Gate, Western Digital, Jobe, and more with this same strategy. Many of my* *writing deals, paid webinars, and speaking engagements all started with a simple tweet.*

#Family selling—Sharon Galor ($$): *We've never spent money on sales and marketing. I've never had a salesperson, and I've never had to pay for advertising. Everything has come from word of mouth. Our marketing is made up of the stories shared by our #Family. Even from our earliest days we grew because the students loved class and would tell all their friends about us. Our #Family of students does all the selling for us.*

#Extraordinary selling—Mark Drager ($$$): *Every touchpoint with a client is an act of sales and marketing. It starts with doing #Extraordinary work with my current clients. This means the client experience and the final product. When a client is blown away throughout the process, they will give referrals. And the great product we produce will attract more. Relationships are everything. I invest to build new relationships and strengthen current ones. This includes regular lunches with current and previous clients. I also sponsor charitable events that my clients care about, or I might handle a pro bono project. The tactics almost don't matter, as long as I'm working with people I want to work with.*

#Joy selling—Richard Sheridan ($$$$): *We don't have a sales team. Menlo has such a compelling story that authors and journalists come here to write about us. Our story has been the cover feature in* Forbes, *the* New York Times, Inc., *and more. We don't need a sales team because clients come to us. If you have an interesting story, and you tell it well, the world helps you share it. We simply tell our story, with passion and enthusiasm, along with the reason behind what we do. And we've received a ridiculous amount of coverage!*

#Honest selling—Christopher Gavigan ($$$$$): *If you want to be the best, you've got to be known for something important. Because we have a personality and point of view in the marketplace, our customers want to help with our mission and be involved with everything we do. So our sales and marketing beats the drum of our ethos and value across the #Honest brand. The heart of sales and marketing is telling your story and what you stand for.*

With all those sales coming in, you're next going to need a way to manage them!

9. PROJECT MANAGEMENT

I learned this . . . when trying to get my high-performance coaching clients to stay on track; the longer their lists of to-dos and goals, the more overwhelmed and off-track they got. Clarity comes with simplicity.

—*Brendon Burchard (the no. 1* New York Times *bestselling author of* The Millionaire Messenger*)*

Projects can get messy and your ability to handle them will make or break your company.

There's a reason why project management has certification programs and has become an important part of every organization.

Project management gets things done.

It gives you a framework to accomplish your goals. It guides you from an idea to a result.

Traditional project management usually involves phases like initiation, planning and design, execution and construction, monitoring and controlling systems, completion and finish point.

There are also many different forms of project management, like PRINCE2, critical chain, process-based, agile, lean, extreme, and benefits realization management.

Your One Word sits on top of your project-management system.

It helps you align your team, not just to a common goal, which is the result of the project, but also to a common way of believing why and how things should get done.

Your One Word is the North Star for your team in everything they do.

If their actions help the project goals but go against your One Word, then they should, at the very least, bring it to your attention.

Your One Word adds a layer of clarity for your team on how to run their projects.

If, for example, your One Word is #Calm and your projects are insanely stressful, then something needs to change.

The team that you attracted based on #Calm will be especially stressed out, won't be happy, and won't deliver an excellent result—even if they follow all the rules set out in traditional project management. When your team is aligned, your projects get finished more effectively.

Here's how I run my projects around #Believe.

#BELIEVE IN YOUR PROJECTS

There are two great days in a person's life—the day we are born and the day we discover why.

—William Barclay (author, radio and television presenter, professor)

For me, project management starts with helping everyone understand why they are doing what they're doing.

I don't want people to be just a cog in the wheel. In most companies, the people behind the scenes don't get to see the results of their work. They don't get to see the happy customers; they don't get invited to receive the awards; they aren't asked to be in the media or give speeches. Not on my team. Before we start any project, I let the people involved know who it's for, why it's important, how valuable they are, how it's going to make a difference in people's lives, and I share regular feedback from the consumers as to how it's helping them. In short, people feel like they are making a difference.

Next it's important to solicit opinions.

If you feel like you're the only one coming up with great ideas in your business, then chances are you're not making people feel comfortable enough or helping them #Believe enough in themselves and their ideas to speak up. Almost every new idea for a project we have goes through at least a few people on my team. Sometimes it also goes to my audience on social media. I solicit feedback. I love new ideas. It not only gives a better end result, it also makes people feel way more involved, recognized, and attached to the success of the project.

Then it's about putting people in the right roles.

Sometimes you have the people already in place. Sometimes you need to hire to bring on the expertise. Sometimes you can bring in an intern or hire someone part time. My favorite way is to stretch a current team member to step outside their comfort zone, #Believe in themselves, and take on a newer, bigger challenge.

Finally it's about creating tasks, deadlines, and working together.

Most of the people on my team have never met each other in person. They're all working from different countries, and yet as soon as they work together on a project for the first time, they quickly fall into a groove. How does this happen when they are in different time zones, have different religious beliefs, different hobbies, different political views, different favorite sports teams, different family situations, etc.? How can they get along and work together so well?

Because they all #Believe. Get your One Word right and it all falls into place.

ONE WORD PROJECT MANAGEMENT

The people who do it are part of the #Family. They grew up from being a student to being the person who coordinates our events.
—*Sharon Galor ($$)*

#Awesome projects—Roberto Blake ($): *I use a variety of tools to help me juggle my activities. Because I do so many activities, I need multiple tools to help me manage effectively. Google Calendar is a big tool for me to set my schedule and give deadlines with notifications. I also use a free task manager called Asana, and I've even hired my sister to "nag" me. Old-school sticky notes are handy too.*

#Family projects—Sharon Galor ($$): *Everyone who's managed the school project is part of the #Family. Anyone who's ever coordinated a project was once a student. Helpers and Instructors will get passionate about a project or event and take the lead. Even the hosts and entertainers of our events are usually students that are energetic about it. We have one primary coordinator to manage the school's schedule. Both times that I hired a coordinator, they were students who wanted more responsibility. They were doing projects for me already, just for* *fun! I expanded their role into a job, and it's worked out beautifully.*

#Extraordinary projects—Mark Drager ($$$): *Communication is the key to effective project management. It's crucial to meet deadlines. I set up a production schedule board on the wall, an idea taken from the television world. There are color-coded cards that display the various stages of production, so my team can easily see the holes in the schedule. Just a glance at the board can quickly tell me how effectively they are progressing through a project or if we need to increase efforts to develop new client business.*

#Joy projects—Richard Sheridan ($$$$): *We manage the weekly work flow with project "story cards." Each project has its own board on our walls. Story cards for each week get pinned onto the board. Story cards are placed into several "swim lanes," with each lane assigned to two people. We put different colored dots next to each task, which represent the stage of completion. This allows anyone to glance at the board and see when we are behind or ahead based on the color dot on the card.*

#Honest projects—Christopher Gavigan ($$$$$): *We put our heads down with #Honest passion and brute force to get things done. Sheer determination and skill have pushed us forward. Sometimes it's not elegant; sometimes it's downright messy. We've done a nice job, however, at a few critical pivot points in our company's growth, at pausing and determining our next direction. As we take care of the consumer, we're listening for project ideas. The customer service team is my direct line to consumer insights and marketing assessment. They give me actionable feedback that I can spin back into the product* *development pipeline. We get ideas for new products, tweaks to marketing, and adjustments to current operations.*

Finally, your One Word will help you make all the tough decisions in your business.

10. TOUGH DECISIONS

It's not hard to make decisions when you know what your values are.

—*Roy E. Disney (longtime senior executive at the Walt Disney Company, founded by his father, Roy, and uncle, Walt Disney)*

Making tough decisions sucks.

It's easy to talk about your One Word and your mission, values, and so on, when things are going well. But what do you do when things are tough? What do you do when you can't pay your rent and someone asks you to do something that goes against your core value but pays really well? Welcome to the world of entrepreneurship.

Your One Word should make tough decisions easier.

You and your business are defined by the decisions you make when things get tough. This is your opportunity to really find out who you are and what you truly believe in.

The CVS Health story:

In the fall of 2014, CVS renamed its business CVS Health and stopped selling cigarettes and tobacco products in all of its 7,700 stores across America. It would cost $2 billion per year in sales, but cigarettes could not exist under its One Word of #Health. As CVS president Larry Merlo said, "While there's never a right time to walk away from $2 billion in revenue, this was the right time . . . Ending the sale of cigarettes and tobacco products at CVS

Pharmacy is simply the right thing to do for the good of our customers and our company. The sale of tobacco products is inconsistent with our purpose—helping people on their path to better health . . . Cigarettes and tobacco products have no place in a setting where health care is delivered. This is the right thing to do."

Talk about a tough decision. Would you walk away from $2 billion per year?

It's easier when you know what you stand for.

CVS then also left the U.S. Chamber of Commerce because it was trying to lobby against antismoking laws. Again, a tough decision that had economic consequences for the company was made easier because of its One Word, #Health. Standing for something important might hurt the company in the short term. Certainly $2 billion doesn't just drop in your lap. But sticking to core values positions you for long-term success. Now customers know what you stand for. Now employees can feel proud. Now the media has something positive to write about.

There is a spillover effect into every area of your business when you stand up for what's right and believe in your decisions even when it costs in the short term.

#BELIEVE IN YOUR DECISIONS

Saying "yes" to one thing means saying "no" to another. That's why decisions can be hard sometimes.

—*Sean Covey (educator, businessman, keynote speaker, and author of* The Seven Habits of Highly Effective People*)*

The hardest decision I ever had to make was when I was nineteen.

Growing up, I thought I'd be a banker. When I played board

games, I was always the banker. Everyone in my family had traditional jobs, and as I've mentioned before, I wrote in my high school yearbook that in ten years, I'd be a VP at a bank.

Then when I was nineteen I was put in an impossible situation.

I became an owner in a software business that wasn't doing very well. While in university, I was making $300 a month and was struggling to get by. I didn't know if entrepreneurship was in the cards for me, and I kept up my studies. Suddenly everything starting going right on my professional career path. I got job opportunities with a leading bank and a leading strategic consulting firm. Job opportunities that my friends drooled over. Job opportunities that flew me to the Waldorf Astoria in New York City for interviews and that promised world travel. Job opportunities that would pay $80,000 to $100,000 starting salaries.

And here I was making three hundred dollars a month with my business.

I didn't know what to do. Should I take the job I thought I always wanted or do this entrepreneurship thing and see it through? Everyone I asked, except my business partners, thought I should take the job. It was safe. It was secure. It was what I always wanted. I'd have money. I'd see the world. Looking back now, it would be easy for me to say that I knew it would all work out and that I rejected those job opportunities without a second thought to focus on my business.

But the reality is that I was scared out of my mind.

What if my company didn't make it? How would I support myself? How could I live with the failure? Would another company even want to hire me? Ultimately I decided to #Believe in myself and not live with regret, wondering what might have happened if I stuck with my business. I had to see it through.

And ever since, I've used the same framework.

I #Believe in myself and ask myself in any tough decision if I'm going to regret saying yes or saying no. If I feel like I'm going to regret it, then I take action. I can live with mistakes. I can live with failure. I can live with being embarrassed.

I don't want to live with regret.

REGRET-FREE ONE WORD DECISIONS

The devil always comes carrying cash. And, man, there was a big pile of cash on the table. And I thought, "Oh, this is going to really hurt to walk away." But it was the right thing to do.

—*Richard Sheridan ($$$$)*

#Awesome decisions—Roberto Blake ($): *I'll turn down a great financial opportunity if it isn't #Awesome. I've refused to work with huge companies, including those in big tobacco, fracking, and most political groups. I'll make some exceptions to this. For example, if a politician is working on a specific cause outside of their campaign, like education, that I'm passionate about.*

#Family decisions—Sharon Galor ($$): *I put #Family first. I once had the opportunity to rent out our studio during the day, but the person who wanted to rent it didn't feel like a good fit. They weren't open and welcoming, and just didn't match our values. When it was time to sign the contract, I backed out of it. I just didn't feel right. I was thinking about the Helpers and how they use the studio to practice, worried that it might interfere with that time. And our Instructors use the space before our regular class, for extra income for themselves from private lessons. I always choose #Family over temporary financial gain.*

#Extraordinary decisions—Mark Drager ($$$): *I rely on my One Word to help me to make tough decisions. I determine what will have the most #Extraordinary outcome, and then I know whether I want to go down that path or not. It helps me have those hard conversations. The team looks to me to show them what it means to be #Extraordinary, and I refuse to do anything less than #Extraordinary. There was a situation where I had a client who had really tight timelines that it just wasn't possible for us to meet. I had to tell him it wasn't possible because the final product would be substandard. I wouldn't sacrifice quality and the client didn't want to pay more.*

#Joy decisions—Richard Sheridan ($$$$): *We can measure #Joy by the delight we're creating out in the world. #Joy is tangible, in that we can track financial results by how well the product is doing in the marketplace. If it's doing well, it's bringing #Joy. We feel it even more directly when we trade cash for equity or royalties in our clients' products. But when #Joy becomes tough, we make tough decisions. We are particular about how we work with clients. We require their involvement, and if customers try to bend us out of #Joy, if they say "It doesn't matter how you do it—just get it done," then we know that they don't care about our moral compass.*

#Honest decisions—Christopher Gavigan ($$$$$): *You have to do what's right for your brand. There have been some situations where vendors aren't living up to our standards. We want them to be side-by-side with us in our mission, but they're not giving us what we need. Often it's because we have grown so quickly. In many case, we've simply outgrown them, and they just can't keep up with our fast pace and scale. We're refining our processes and have demands on more engagement and regulatory requirements. And* *some folks just can't handle it. It's hard to end our relationship because we've built our brand alongside of some of these folks!*

CHAPTER 7 HIGHLIGHTS

IMPORTANT TAKEAWAYS

- How you treat clients matters. Once you sell something to someone, you've got to manage the relationship. Every single interaction with a client should come from your One Word, and the strategies you use to communicate should also be One Word driven.
- Your suppliers represent your brand. It's about working with businesses who understand what you stand for and believe in the same thing. The more closely aligned you are, the more they are going to help you grow.
- The way most businesses choose new products and services is flawed. You need to make the big decisions with your heart and the little ones with your head. Let your heart guide your big decisions, then use your head to figure out how to do it.
- You need to be proud of the products and services you create. If you want people to care about your products, then you need to show you care about them first.
- Research and development helps you accomplish your impossible goals. If you can show people that the work they are doing is changing lives, they'll give you not just their minds but their hearts and souls as well.
- The people you surround yourself with matter. Advisors are there to push you. When you're clear about what you stand for, you'll attract advisors who love you.

- You don't want just anybody's money. Bringing money isn't enough. The ideal investor should bring you everything: Capital. Connections. Ideas. Resources. And a shared set of values.
- The traditional salesperson needs to evolve . . . or they will die.
- Projects can get messy and your ability to handle them will make or break your company. Your One Word sits on top of your project-management system and adds a layer of clarity for your team on how to run their projects.
- Making tough decisions sucks. Your One Word should make tough decisions easier. There is a spillover effect into every area of your business when you stand up for what's right even though it might not make short-term financial sense.

CONCLUSION

The biggest barrier to starting a company isn't ideas, funding, or experience. It's excuses.

—*Sarah Lacy (technology journalist and author)*

THIS BOOK IS NOT A BOOK

Everybody that's successful lays a blueprint out.

—*Kevin Hart (actor and comedian)*

This isn't just another book. It's a blueprint.

When I started on my One Word path, I thought I was crazy.

I thought it was too big, too bold, too risky. Then once I decided, I figured I'd have to stumble my way through it, just following my instincts and what I felt was right. After all, nobody else was doing this and there was no book to follow.

Until I found others who were doing it. They built full-time businesses for themselves all the way up to multibillion-dollar empires.

And what I discovered was that they didn't have all the answers either. They stumbled their way through it, just following their instincts and doing what they felt was right. They didn't have a book to follow.

So I combined their stories, lessons learned, and insights and wrote the book so doing it would be easier for you. I traveled across North America to go visit them so you didn't have to. I condensed hours upon hours of conversations into their most essential parts to give you the plan for success.

You now have the blueprint to build something important— thanks to years of trial and error by these successful entrepreneurs.

I wish someone had done this work for me. I wish I'd had this template to follow when I was starting. It would have shaved a lot of time and money off my learning curve and sped up my ability to create the business I really wanted.

But it's said the best business ideas are the ones that come from solving your own problems. If you're facing an important issue and fix it, chances are there are many others who have the same problem and would love a solution.

So I hope you take the knowledge in this book and apply it. Immediately. I hope you leverage the efforts that others went through to get this far and create something amazing for yourself and this planet. I hope you take it seriously, because when you apply the strategies in this book you will changes lives.

Core. Campaign. Company. Follow the steps in order to make it as easy as possible for you to succeed.

It all starts with your Core.

YOUR ONE WORD IS YOUR CORE

I think it's very important not to do what your peers think you should do, not do what your parents think you should do, or your teachers or even your culture. Do what's inside of you.

—*George Lucas (billionaire entrepreneur and creator of* Star Wars *and* Indiana Jones*)*

Stop being mediocre.

Most people live mediocre lives and have set the bar so low for themselves that they've created a world where it's okay to be mediocre. The people you hang out with, the websites you visit, the media you consume—everything in your environment holds you exactly where you are. You need to find your greatness. Everyone starts at the start. The difference is where you see yourself going.

You have One Word.

There is One Word that defines who you are, connects all the things in your life that make you come alive, and will help you escape the chains of mediocrity. People want to know who you are and what you stand for before they'll buy anything from you. Make your cause be your customer's cause too. Forget features and benefits. They work but they're not efficient. The real gold is in Core Selling. Making money is so much more than just having a great product or service. It's about how you make people feel when they see your brand. If money is your only goal, you'll never be rich. You have to want to have an impact and leave a legacy. Your One Word is also more than a marketing slogan. It's a way of life. When you know your One Word, you can make decisions that support your path. The One Word philosophy has helped entrepreneurs generate millions in sales and it can work for you too.

How to find your One Word

Finding your One Word is one of the most important exercises you will ever do in your life. If you want to succeed, then you need to start with what makes you happy. Find the common theme from the list of things that make you happy and write it down. This is where the magic starts to happen. If you don't know who you are, then start by thinking of who you aren't. Make a list of everything and everyone that makes you unhappy, and figure out what binds them together. Your One Word is not a New Year's resolution. It's a constant. It's not something you get bored of.

Your core value, your One Word, doesn't change. Your One Word is supposed to be bold. The story you tell yourself about what you can't do has hurt you for your entire life. Be bold and be proud. Don't talk it over more with others. Talk with yourself more. Stop being ruled by the opinions and judgments of other people. This is your life. Live it. You don't need anyone's permission. The more powerful a word you pick, the more it will have been used by others. The unique part isn't the word but your take on it.

Now that you know what you stand for, you can create a powerful Campaign around it to inspire others to take action.

BUILD AN INSPIRING CAMPAIGN

There are many elements to a campaign. Leadership is number one. Everything else is number two.

—*Bertolt Brecht (poet, playwright, and theater director)*

Your One Word can change the world.

One individual can start a movement that turns the tide of history. When you give people an opportunity to be a part of something important, they jump on board. Start with a simple test and prove to yourself that your One Word has power. You don't have to spend months planning—just find something easy and start! I had 50 percent better results in one month with a #Believe video than I did with my old video, which took an entire year to break the hundred-thousand-view barrier. When you stand for something powerful, something that means something to you, something that other people can easily understand, people will share it and rally behind you. You owe it to yourself to try so you don't have any regrets later in life. You rarely regret the things that you try and fail at, and the upside is you get to live your dreams. If you're not motivated, you won't create great work. Ask yourself: What do I hate about being an employee? Why did I start? and What do I want to be remembered for?

How to build a powerful campaign

You don't need all of these elements to be successful. Many people succeed with only a few. But the more you incorporate into your campaign, the greater your chances are of creating a powerful movement. Start with a credo to energize you and the people you reach. Your credo is the inspiration behind everything you create. Your founding story is also important. Way more important than you likely give it credit for. Your story adds value and context to your customers. Most people's bios are boring. Superboring. Make yours interesting. Make it personal. Make me care about you. It works for me. It can work for you. Next, connect a loyal fan base to yourself, your business, your cause, and each other. Name them. Recognize them. Bring them together. Give them rituals. Then think about your company name. Chances are you were given the wrong advice about how to choose a name for your business. Your name should mean more than just what you sell. It should be flexible. Having an enemy is a catalyst for action. Find your enemy and create a rallying cry for positive change. Symbols are also important components of any campaign. What symbol represents your enemy? How about One Word? Colors have meaning too. Fonts make you feel. Music is language, and it can be used to make people connect to your business. And none of this has to cost you a lot of money. If you can combine a powerful purpose with these elements that help tell a story, you'll be well on your way to building a lasting, impactful, world-changing brand.

Finally you're ready to turn your Campaign into a Company that can make an even greater impact and reach more people.

ONE WORD COMPANY BUILDING

> I really try and live the mission of the company and . . . keep
> everything else in my life extremely simple.
>
> —*Mark Zuckerberg (founder of Facebook)*

Build a company culture around your One Word.

The team you build will make or break your company. Your One Word is the essential ingredient that binds them together. Hire misfits who are perfect fits for you, and attract them using your One Word. If you do a good job hiring, you shouldn't need to do a lot of onboarding. You've already taken care of it in your hiring process. Next, look at your working environment. Your environment holds you where you are. If you want to be great, you have to surround yourself with greatness. Does your environment transport you to a different world that people can't wait to come back to? Next create rituals to build and reinforce the culture you are creating. They define your business. The strongest cultures also create their own language. Make your names powerful. Fill them with meaning, and your team will respond accordingly. When you have a strong culture based on your One Word, you don't need many strict policies. Your One Word should direct the plans, decisions, and actions of your team. Finally, firing people sucks. Just like when you're hiring people, when you're firing people your One Word should help you make the decision. If they have the skills but not the alignment, your One Word will give you clarity about what's best for your business.

Use your One Word to guide your business operations.

Start with your clients. Once you sell something to someone, you've got to manage the relationship. Every single interaction with a client should come from your One Word, and the strategies you use to communicate should also be One Word driven. Move on to your suppliers. It's about working with businesses that get what you stand for and believe in the same thing. The more closely aligned you are, the more they are going to help you grow. Then think about new products and services. You need to be proud of the products and services you create. If you want people to care about your products, you need to show you care about them first. You can move on to apply your One Word to your research and development, advisory team, investors, salespeople, and project management. Since it is your core value, it touches every part of the business. Finally, making tough decisions sucks. Your One Word should make tough decisions easier. There is a spillover effect into every area of your business when you stand up for what's right even though it might not make short-term financial or logical sense.

You have all the ingredients for success. But it won't make a difference unless you act.

YOU NEED TO ACT

A real decision is measured by the fact that you've taken a new action. If there's no action, you haven't truly decided.

—*Tony Robbins (life coach, self-help author, and motivational speaker)*

Okay, great, so you finished another book.

For some of you this might actually be a major accomplishment—that is, if you don't typically read books. Congrats! For others, maybe you're reading a book a week and you've added this to your "completed" list and put it on your bookshelf. Either way, it's not enough.

Just reading any book—but especially this book!—is not enough.

If all you've done so far is read, then we're all wasting our time.

My time was wasted in researching and writing for the past year and your time was wasted for however long it took you to read this book.

You. Need. To. Act.

Here's one of the most important things I've ever learned about goal setting: once you set a goal, you need to take *immediate* action toward doing something to achieve it.

It doesn't have to be a big, bold action. Just something. Send an e-mail. Commit to a friend. Post on your Facebook account. Something. Anything. Just get the momentum going. Because when you say "tomorrow," I know you have every intention of doing it tomorrow, but then tomorrow comes and it gets pushed to the next day, and then the next day, and then you just forget about it—and your life continues on as it always has, without any major changes happening.

Stop it.

Yes, "it's late." Or you don't "have the time" right now. Or you want to "make sure that it's perfect" before you start. *Stop. It.* There is no perfect time or perfect place to start. There is always going to be an excuse. You're a smart person, so you have created really smart reasons why you can't start right now.

Here's the thing: it's way more important to do *something* right now than to do the *perfect thing* later. Because there is no perfect thing. And you likely won't do anything later.

So get started today. Right now. Act. Feel the strength and power that the momentum brings you.

"That's great, but, Evan, you don't understand . . ."

"BUT, EVAN . . ."

People spend too much time finding other people to blame, too much energy finding excuses for not being what they are capable of

being, and not enough energy putting themselves on the line,
growing out of the past, and getting on with their lives.

—*J. Michael Straczynski (writer and producer, known for writing the* Thor,
Superman, *and* Superman: Earth One *graphic novels)*

"Evan, you don't get it. I'm . . ."

This is perhaps the biggest roadblock of all for you: The story
you tell yourself that holds you back. Go look at yourself in the
mirror and ask why you aren't as successful as you'd like to be?
What does the voice inside your head say? Here are some common answers:

I'm not successful because . . .

- I don't have the resources
- I don't have the right connections
- I didn't get the right (or any) education
- My parents aren't successful
- My government holds me back
- I'm a minority / woman / too young / too old / disabled
- I don't deserve it
- I won't be able to sustain it
- I'm not creative / outgoing / an expert / a techie / good with people
- Someone else is already doing it
- People will judge me if I try and fail

Meanwhile, there are people who come from worse backgrounds than you and are chasing their dreams and making things happen.

The point isn't to just ignore these reasons. Sure, if you grew
up in Somalia and had to deal with civil wars, prolonged

droughts, and pirates, it *will* be much tougher for you than for someone from a middle-class family in New York City.

But so what?

That's the hand you were dealt. What are you going to do about it? Continue to blame other people forever? Or take some responsibility for your own life? The fact that you picked up this book means you can read. You understand English. It likely means you have Internet access. You have a roof over your head, and you have many other advantages that others don't. The people who change the world understand that it's never about how many resources you have: it's about how resourceful you are. It's about how you use what you do have. It's about being grateful for what's in your life and taking responsibility for what's to come.

It's nobody else's fault. It's up to you to make it happen.

IT'S UP TO YOU

Life's too short to hang out with people who aren't resourceful.

—*Jeff Bezos (billionaire founder of Amazon.com)*

John Paul DeJoria's parents divorced when he was two.

When he was nine, he sold newspapers and Christmas cards door-to-door to help his family. When his single mother wasn't able to support him anymore, he was sent to live in a foster home in Los Angeles, where he joined a gang and where his high school math teacher told him he would "never succeed at anything in life." His later jobs included being a janitor and an insurance salesman. Today he's a billionaire.

Oprah Winfrey was originally named Orpah, but people mispronounced it so often that she kept the name Oprah.

She was born to an unmarried teenage mother who worked as

a maid. She spent the first years of her life in poverty and was so poor that she often wore dresses made of potato sacks and the local kids teased her about it. She was molested by her cousin, uncle, and family friend when she was nine. At thirteen she ran away from home and at fourteen had a child, who died prematurely. At the time of this writing, she is currently North America's first and only multibillionaire black person.

When Abraham Lincoln was nine years old, his mother died from an illness.

He was formally educated for less than one year. He gave all the income he earned to his father until he was twenty-one. The first love of his life died when he was twenty-two. Three of the four children he had died before they reached adulthood. His wife was eventually committed to a mental health asylum, and he suffered from "melancholy," now referred to as clinical depression. In his political career he was defeated eight times trying to be everything from a congressman to senator to vice president. In 1860 he won the election to become president of the United States and is now considered to be one of the greatest presidents in American history.

How do their stories compare to yours?

It's hard to imagine that you have less support than John Paul DeJoria had, fewer resources than Oprah Winfrey had, or more personal setbacks than Abraham Lincoln had.

You have in this book, and inside you, the tools you need to succeed. It's up to you to act. Act boldly. For your sake and the world's.

#Believe

ACKNOWLEDGMENTS

I'd like to acknowledge you, the reader.

The you who bought this book. You're in for a heck of a ride. Thank you for supporting me.

The you who bought multiple copies of this book to gift to friends. You understand that the secret to living is giving. Thank you from me and your friends for being an amazing human being.

The you who bootlegged this book. Please consider supporting authors who impact your life. Thank you for your future support.

The you who buys books but never reads them. Stop collecting books and start collecting knowledge. Thank you for the future impact you'll have when you start reading.

The you who reads a book a day but doesn't take action. Slow down, absorb, and apply what you read. Thank you for the future impact you'll have when you start applying.

The you who reads this book but is afraid to take action. Stop living someone else's dream and start betting on yourself. Thank you for having the courage to pick up this book and explore your unlimited self.

The you who reads this book and takes immediate action. You're the 1 percent who change the world. Thank you for your making this planet better—it's an honor for me to be a part of your journey.

ABOUT THE AUTHOR

I #Believe in entrepreneurs.

At nineteen, I built then sold a biotech software company.

At twenty-two, I was a VC helping raise $500,000 to $15 million.

I now run EvanCarmichael.com, a popular website for entrepreneurs.

I breathe and bleed entrepreneurship.

I'm obsessed.

Aiming to help one billion entrepreneurs.

Change the world.

I've set two world records, use a stand-up desk, ride a Vespa, raise funds for Kiva, wear five-toe shoes, and created Entrepreneur trading cards.

I speak globally but Toronto (#EntCity) is home.

I love being married, my son, salsa dancing, DJing, League of Legends, and the Toronto Blue Jays.